The UK
TOWER AIR FRYER
Cookbook

Everyday Recipes for Beginners,

The Best Guide for

Beginners to Professionals

Glenn Jiles

CONTENTS

Chapter 3 Beef ，pork & Lamb Recipes 30

Chapter 4 Fish And Seafood Recipes 40

Chapter 5 Vegetarians Recipes 50

Chapter 6 Vegetable Side Dishes Recipes 60

Chapter 7 Appetizers And Snacks 70

Chapter 8 Sandwiches And Burgers Recipes 80

Chapter 9 Desserts And Sweets 91

INDEX 101

INTRODUCTION

The Tower Air Fryer is an easy way to cook delicious healthy meals. Rather than cooking the food in oil and hot fat that may affect your health, the machine uses rapid hot air to circulate around and cook meals. This allows the outside of your food to be crispy and also makes sure that the inside layers are cooked through.

Tower Air Fryer allows us to cook almost everything and a lot of dishes. We can use the Tower air Fryer to cook Meat, vegetables, poultry, fruit, fish and a wide variety of desserts. It is possible to prepare your entire meals, starting from appetizers to main courses as well as desserts. Not to mention, Tower air fryer also allows home prepared preserves or even delicious sweets and cakes.

How Does Tower Air Fryer Works?

The technology of the Tower Air Fryer is very simple. Fried foods get their crunchy texture because hot oil heats foods quickly and evenly on their surface. Oil is an excellent heat conductor, which helps with fast and simultaneous cooking across all of the ingredients. For decades cooks have used convection ovens to try to mimic the effects of frying or cooking the whole surface of food. But the air never circulates quickly enough to achieve that delicious surface crisp we all love in fried foods.

With this mechanism the air is circulated on high degrees, up to 200° C, to "air fry" any food such as fish, chicken or chips etc. This technology has changed the whole idea of cooking by reducing the fat up to 80% compared to old-fashioned deep fat frying.

The Tower air fryer cooking releases the heat through a heating element which cooks the food in a healthier and more appropriate way. There's also an exhaust fan right above the cooking chamber which provides the food required airflow. This way food is cooked with constant heated air. This leads to the same heating temperature reaching every single part of the food that is being cooked. So, this is only grill and the exhaust fan that is helping the Tower air fryer to boost air at a constantly high speed in order to cook healthy food with less fat.

The internal pressure increases the temperature that will then be controlled by the exhaust system. Exhaust fan also releases filtered extra air to cook the food in a much healthier way. Tower air fryer has no odor at all and it is absolutely harmless making it user and environment friendly.

Advantages

VORTX TECHNOLOGY:

Rapid air circulation cooks 30% faster with 99% less oil and the same delicious fried crispiness and taste – you lose the fat, not the flavour

99% LESS FAT:

It uses only minimal oil to make mealtimes healthier, cooking all of your favourite fried food with 99% less fat

SAVE UP TO 50% ON ENERGY:

Cooking food 30% faster, Tower Air Fryer use less power than conventional ovens. Save on up to 50% on your energy by simply switching to Air Fryer cooking

FOOD COOKS FASTER:

Cooks food faster than a standard oven so you don't have to spend as much time in the kitchen. You can create deliciously-crisp and golden chips in just 15 minutes

COOKING MADE SIMPLE:

It's easy to adjust the cooking temperature (up to 200 degrees) and set the 30-minute timer using the dial controls, ensuring perfectly-cooked results from the first use

EASY CLEANING:

The non-stick crisper tray can be removed from the air fryer and washed with warm, soapy water to easily take care of the cleaning

Cleaning & Care

WARNING! DO NOT IMMERSE THE APPLIANCE IN WATER OR ANY OTHER LIQUID.Clean the appliance after every use.Cleaning the pan and the non-stick coating basket:1. Do not use metal kitchen utensils or abrasive cleaning materials to clean the pan or basket, as this may damage the non-stick coating.2. Remove the mains plug from the wall socket and let the appliance cool down before cleaning it.Note: Removing the pan allows the Air Fryer to cool down quicker.3. Wipe the outside of the appliance with a moist cloth.4. Clean the pan, separator and basket with hot water, some washing-up liquid and a non-abrasive sponge.5. You can use degreasing liquid to remove any remaining dirt.Note: the pan and basket are hand-wash only. DO NOT place any part of this appliance in the dishwasher.6. Tip: If dirt is stuck to the basket or the bottom of the pan, fill the pan with hot water with some washing-up liquid. Put the basket in the pan and let the pan and the basket soak for approximately 10 minutes.7. Clean the inside of the appliance with hot water and a non-abrasive sponge.8. Clean the heating element with a cleaning brush to remove any food residues.To store your appliance:• Ensure that the grill is cool, clean and dry before you store it. • Store the appliance in a cool and dry place.

Chapter 1 Bread And Breakfast

Peppered Maple Bacon Knots

Servings: 6

Cooking Time: 8 Minutes

Ingredients:

- 1 pound maple smoked center-cut bacon
- ¼ cup maple syrup
- ¼ cup brown sugar
- coarsely cracked black peppercorns

Directions:

1. Tie each bacon strip in a loose knot and place them on a baking sheet.
2. Combine the maple syrup and brown sugar in a bowl. Brush each knot generously with this mixture and sprinkle with coarsely cracked black pepper.
3. Preheat the air fryer to 390°F.
4. Air-fry the bacon knots in batches. Place one layer of knots in the air fryer basket and air-fry for 5 minutes. Turn the bacon knots over and air-fry for an additional 3 minutes.
5. Serve warm.

Crispy Samosa Rolls

Servings: 4

Cooking Time: 30 Minutes

Ingredients:

- 2/3 cup canned peas
- 4 scallions, finely sliced
- 2 cups grated potatoes
- 2 tbsp lemon juice
- 1 tsp ground ginger
- 1 tsp curry powder
- 1 tsp Garam masala
- ¼ cup chickpea flour
- 1 tbsp tahini
- 8 rice paper wrappers

Directions:

1. Preheat air fryer to 350°F. Mix the peas, scallions, potatoes, lemon juice, ginger, curry powder, Garam masala, and chickpea flour in a bowl. In another bowl, whisk tahini and 1/3 cup of water until combined. Set aside on a plate.
2. Submerge the rice wrappers, one by one, into the tahini mixture until they begin to soften and set aside on a plate.
3. Fill each wrap with 1/3 cup of the veggie mixture and wrap them into a roll. Bake for 15 minutes until golden brown and crispy, turning once. Serve right away.

Crunchy Granola Muffins

Servings:4
Cooking Time: 15 Minutes
Ingredients:
- 1 cup walnut pieces
- 1 cup sunflower seeds
- 1 cup coconut flakes
- ¼ cup granulated sugar
- ⅛ cup coconut flour
- ⅛ cup pecan flour
- 2 tsp ground cinnamon
- 2 tbsp melted butter
- 2 tbsp almond butter
- ⅛ tsp salt

Directions:

1. Preheat air fryer to 300ºF. In a bowl, mix the walnuts, sunflower seeds, coconut flakes, sugar, coconut flour, pecan flour, cinnamon, butter, almond butter, and salt.
2. Spoon the mixture into an ungreased round 4-cup baking dish. Place it in the frying basket and Bake for 6 minutes, stirring once. Transfer to an airtight container, let cool for 10 minutes, then cover and store at room temperature until ready to serve.

Lemon Monkey Bread

Servings: 4
Cooking Time: 15 Minutes
Ingredients:
- 1 can refrigerated biscuits
- ¼ cup white sugar
- 3 tbsp brown sugar
- ½ tsp ground cinnamon
- 1 lemon, zested
- ¼ tsp ground nutmeg
- 3 tbsp melted butter

Directions:

1. Preheat air fryer to 350°F. Take the biscuits out of the can and separate them. Cut each biscuit into 4 equal pieces. In a bowl, mix white sugar, brown sugar, lemon zest, cinnamon, and nutmeg. Have the melted butter nearby. Dip each biscuit piece into the butter, then roll into the cinnamon sugar until coated. Place in a baking pan. Bake in the air fryer until golden brown, 6-9 minutes. Let cool for 5 minutes before serving as the sugar will be hot.

Garlic-cheese Biscuits

Servings: 8
Cooking Time: 8 Minutes
Ingredients:

- 1 cup self-rising flour
- 1 teaspoon garlic powder
- 2 tablespoons butter, diced
- 2 ounces sharp Cheddar cheese, grated
- ½ cup milk
- cooking spray

Directions:

1. Preheat air fryer to 330°F.
2. Combine flour and garlic in a medium bowl and stir together.
3. Using a pastry blender or knives, cut butter into dry ingredients.
4. Stir in cheese.
5. Add milk and stir until stiff dough forms.
6. If dough is too sticky to handle, stir in 1 or 2 more tablespoons of self-rising flour before shaping. Biscuits should be firm enough to hold their shape. Otherwise, they'll stick to the air fryer basket.
7. Divide dough into 8 portions and shape into 2-inch biscuits about ¾-inch thick.
8. Spray air fryer basket with nonstick cooking spray.
9. Place all 8 biscuits in basket and cook at 330°F for 8 minutes.

Chicken Scotch Eggs

Servings:4
Cooking Time: 25 Minutes
Ingredients:

- 1 lb ground chicken
- 2 tsp Dijon mustard
- 2 tsp grated yellow onion
- 1 tbsp chopped chives
- 1 tbsp chopped parsley
- ⅛ tsp ground nutmeg
- 1 lemon, zested
- Salt and pepper to taste
- 4 hard-boiled eggs, peeled
- 1 egg, beaten
- 1 cup bread crumbs
- 2 tsp olive oil

Directions:

1. Preheat air fryer to 350ºF. In a bowl, mix the ground chicken, mustard, onion, chives, parsley, nutmeg, salt, lemon zest and pepper. Shape into 4 oval balls and form the balls evenly around the boiled eggs. Submerge them in the beaten egg and dip in the crumbs. Brush with olive oil. Place the scotch eggs in the frying basket and Air Fry for 14 minutes, flipping once. Serve hot.

Veggie & Feta Scramble Bowls

Servings: 2

Cooking Time: 25 Minutes

Ingredients:

- 1 russet potato, cubed
- 1 bell pepper, cut into strips
- ½ feta, cubed
- 1 tbsp nutritional yeast
- ½ tsp garlic powder
- ½ tsp onion powder
- ¼ tsp ground turmeric
- 1 tbsp apple cider vinegar

Directions:

1. Preheat air fryer to 400°F. Put in potato cubes and bell pepper strips and Air Fry for 10 minutes. Combine the feta, nutritional yeast, garlic, onion, turmeric, and apple vinegar in a small pan. Fit a trivet in the fryer, lay the pan on top, and Air Fry for 5 more minutes until potatoes are tender and feta cheese cooked. Share potatoes and bell peppers into 2 bowls and top with feta scramble. Serve.

English Scones

Servings: 8

Cooking Time: 8 Minutes

Ingredients:

- 2 cups all-purpose flour
- 1 tablespoon baking powder
- ½ teaspoon salt
- 2 tablespoons sugar
- ¼ cup unsalted butter
- ⅔ cup plus 1 tablespoon whole milk, divided

Directions:

1. Preheat the air fryer to 380°F.
2. In a large bowl, whisk together the flour, baking powder, salt, and sugar. Using a pastry blender or your fingers, cut in the butter until pea-size crumbles appear. Make a well in the center and pour in ⅔ cup of the milk. Quickly mix the batter until a ball forms. Knead the dough 3 times.
3. Place the dough onto a floured surface and, using your hands or a rolling pin, flatten the dough until it's ¾ inch thick. Using a biscuit cutter or drinking glass, cut out 10 circles, reforming the dough and flattening as needed to use up the batter.
4. Brush the tops lightly with the remaining 1 tablespoon of milk.
5. Place the scones into the air fryer basket. Cook for 8 minutes or until golden brown and cooked in the center.

Hole In One

Servings: 1
Cooking Time: 7 Minutes
Ingredients:

- 1 slice bread
- 1 teaspoon soft butter
- 1 egg
- salt and pepper
- 1 tablespoon shredded Cheddar cheese
- 2 teaspoons diced ham

Directions:

1. Place a 6 x 6-inch baking dish inside air fryer basket and preheat fryer to 330°F.
2. Using a 2½-inch-diameter biscuit cutter, cut a hole in center of bread slice.
3. Spread softened butter on both sides of bread.
4. Lay bread slice in baking dish and crack egg into the hole. Sprinkle egg with salt and pepper to taste.
5. Cook for 5minutes.
6. Turn toast over and top it with shredded cheese and diced ham.
7. Cook for 2 more minutes or until yolk is done to your liking.

Lemon-blueberry Morning Bread

Servings:2
Cooking Time: 15 Minutes
Ingredients:

- ½ cup flour
- ¼ cup powdered sugar
- ½ tsp baking powder
- ⅛ tsp salt
- 2 tbsp butter, melted
- 1 egg
- ½ tsp gelatin
- ½ tsp vanilla extract
- 1 tsp lemon zest
- ½ cup blueberries

Directions:

1. Preheat air fryer to 300°F. Mix the flour, sugar, baking powder, and salt in a bowl. In another bowl, whisk the butter, egg, gelatin, lemon zest, vanilla extract, and blueberries. Add egg mixture to flour mixture and stir until smooth. Spoon mixture into a pizza pan. Place pan in the frying basket and Bake for 10 minutes. Let sit for 5 minutes before slicing. Serve immediately.

Mediterranean Granola

Servings: 6
Cooking Time: 40 Minutes

Ingredients:

- 1 cup rolled oats
- ¼ cup dried cherries, diced
- ¼ cup almond slivers
- ¼ cup hazelnuts, chopped
- ¼ cup pepitas
- ¼ cup hemp hearts
- 3 tbsp honey
- 1 tbsp olive oil
- 1 tsp ground cinnamon
- ¼ tsp ground nutmeg
- ¼ tsp salt
- 2 tbsp dark chocolate chips
- 3 cups Greek yogurt

Directions:

1. Preheat air fryer to 260°F. Stir the oats, cherries, almonds, hazelnuts, pepitas, hemp hearts, 2 tbsp of honey, olive oil, cinnamon, nutmeg, and salt in a bowl, mixing well. Pour the mixture onto the parchment-lined frying basket and spread it into a single layer. Bake for 25-30 minutes, shaking twice. Let the granola cool completely. Stir in the chocolate chips. Divide between 6 cups. Top with Greek yogurt and remaining honey to serve.

Mediterranean Egg Sandwich

Servings: 1
Cooking Time: 8 Minutes

Ingredients:

- 1 large egg
- 5 baby spinach leaves, chopped
- 1 tablespoon roasted bell pepper, chopped
- 1 English muffin
- 1 thin slice prosciutto or Canadian bacon

Directions:

1. Spray a ramekin with cooking spray or brush the inside with extra-virgin olive oil.
2. In a small bowl, whisk together the egg, baby spinach, and bell pepper.
3. Split the English muffin in half and spray the inside lightly with cooking spray or brush with extra-virgin olive oil.
4. Preheat the air fryer to 350°F for 2 minutes. Place the egg ramekin and open English muffin into the air fryer basket, and cook at 350°F for 5 minutes. Open the air fryer drawer and add the prosciutto or bacon; cook for an additional 1 minute.
5. To assemble the sandwich, place the egg on one half of the English muffin, top with prosciutto or bacon, and place the remaining piece of English muffin on top.

Cheesy Egg Bites

Servings: 6

Cooking Time: 35 Minutes

Ingredients:

- ½ cup shredded Muenster cheese
- 5 eggs, beaten
- 3 tbsp sour cream
- ½ tsp dried oregano
- Salt and pepper to taste
- 1/3 cup minced bell pepper
- 3 tbsp minced scallions

Directions:

1. Preheat the air fryer to 325°F. Make a foil sling: Fold an 18-inch-long piece of heavy-duty aluminum foil lengthwise into thirds. Combine the eggs, sour cream, oregano, salt, and pepper in a bowl. Add the bell peppers, scallions, and cheese and stir. Add the mixture to 6 egg bite cups, making sure to get some of the solids in each cup.

2. Put the egg bite pan on the sling you made and lower it into the fryer. Leave the foil in but bend down the edges so they fit. Bake the bites for 10-15 minutes or until a toothpick inserted into the center comes out clean. Remove the egg bite pan using the foil sling. Cool for 5 minutes, then turn the pan upside down over a plate to remove the egg bites. Serve warm.

Avocado Toasts With Poached Eggs

Servings: 4

Cooking Time: 15 Minutes

Ingredients:

- 4 eggs
- Salt and pepper to taste
- 4 bread pieces, toasted
- 1 pitted avocado, sliced
- ½ tsp chili powder
- ½ tsp dried rosemary

Directions:

1. Preheat air fryer to 320°F. Crack 1 egg into each greased ramekin and season with salt and black pepper. Place the ramekins into the air frying basket. Bake for 6-8 minutes.

2. Scoop the flesh of the avocado into a small bowl. Season with salt, black pepper, chili powderp and rosemary. Using a fork, smash the avocado lightly. Spread the smashed avocado evenly over toasted bread slices. Remove the eggs from the air fryer and gently spoon one onto each slice of avocado toast. Serve and enjoy!

Crunchy French Toast Sticks

Servings: 2

Cooking Time: 9 Minutes

Ingredients:

- 2 eggs, beaten
- ¾ cup milk
- ½ teaspoon vanilla extract
- ½ teaspoon ground cinnamon
- 1½ cups crushed crunchy cinnamon cereal, or any cereal flakes
- 4 slices Texas Toast (or other bread that you can slice into 1-inch thick slices)
- maple syrup, for serving
- vegetable oil or melted butter

Directions:

1. Combine the eggs, milk, vanilla and cinnamon in a shallow bowl. Place the crushed cereal in a second shallow bowl.
2. Trim the crusts off the slices of bread and cut each slice into 3 sticks. Dip the sticks of bread into the egg mixture, turning them over to coat all sides. Let the bread sticks absorb the egg mixture for ten seconds or so, but don't let them get too wet. Roll the bread sticks in the cereal crumbs, pressing the cereal gently onto all sides so that it adheres to the bread.
3. Preheat the air fryer to 400°F.
4. Spray or brush the air fryer basket with oil or melted butter. Place the coated sticks in the basket. It's ok to stack a few on top of the others in the opposite direction.
5. Air-fry for 9 minutes. Turn the sticks over a couple of times during the cooking process so that the sticks crisp evenly. Serve warm with the maple syrup or some berries.

Mini Bacon Egg Quiches

Servings:6

Cooking Time: 30 Minutes

Ingredients:

- 3 eggs
- 2 tbsp heavy cream
- ¼ tsp Dijon mustard
- Salt and pepper to taste
- 3 oz cooked bacon, crumbled
- ¼ cup grated cheddar

Directions:

1. Preheat air fryer to 350ºF. Beat the eggs with salt and pepper in a bowl until fluffy. Stir in heavy cream, mustard, cooked bacon, and cheese. Divide the mixture between 6 greased muffin cups and place them in the frying basket. Bake for 8-10 minutes. Let cool slightly before serving.

Shakshuka Cups

Servings: 4

Cooking Time: 25 Minutes

Ingredients:

- 2 tbsp tomato paste
- ½ cup chicken broth
- 4 tomatoes, diced
- 2 garlic cloves, minced
- ½ tsp dried oregano
- ½ tsp dried coriander
- ½ tsp dried basil
- ¼ tsp red pepper flakes
- ¼ tsp paprika
- 4 eggs
- Salt and pepper to taste
- 2 scallions, diced
- ½ cup grated cheddar cheese
- ½ cup Parmesan cheese
- 4 bread slices, toasted

Directions:

1. Preheat air fryer to 350°F. Combine the tomato paste, chicken broth, tomatoes, garlic, oregano, coriander, basil, red pepper flakes, and paprika. Pour the mixture evenly into greased ramekins. Bake in the air fryer for 5 minutes. Carefully remove the ramekins and crack one egg in each ramekin, then season with salt and pepper. Top with scallions, grated cheese, and Parmesan cheese. Return the ramekins to the frying basket and bake for 3-5 minutes until the eggs are set, and the cheese is melted. Serve with toasted bread immediately.

Chili Hash Browns

Servings: 4

Cooking Time: 45 Minutes

Ingredients:

- 1 tbsp ancho chili powder
- 1 tbsp chipotle powder
- 2 tsp ground cumin
- 2 tsp smoked paprika
- 1 tsp garlic powder
- 1 tsp cayenne pepper
- Salt and pepper to taste
- 2 peeled russet potatoes, grated
- 2 tbsp olive oil
- 1/3 cup chopped onion
- 3 garlic cloves, minced

Directions:

1. Preheat the air fryer to 400°F. Combine chili powder, cumin, paprika, garlic powder, chipotle, cayenne, and black pepper in a small bowl, then pour into a glass jar with a lid and store in a cool, dry place. Add the olive oil, onion, and garlic to a cake pan, put it in the air fryer, and Bake for 3 minutes. Put the grated potatoes in a bowl and sprinkle with 2 tsp of the spice mixture, toss and add them to the cake pan along with the onion mix. Bake for 20-23 minutes, stirring once or until the potatoes are crispy and golden. Season with salt and serve.

Green Egg Quiche

Servings: 4

Cooking Time: 30 Minutes

Ingredients:

- 1 cup broccoli florets
- 2 cups baby spinach
- 2 garlic cloves, minced
- ¼ tsp ground nutmeg
- 1 tbsp olive oil
- Salt and pepper to taste
- 4 eggs
- 2 scallions, chopped
- 1 red onion, chopped
- 1 tbsp sour cream
- ½ cup grated fontina cheese

Directions:

1. Preheat air fryer to 375°F. Combine broccoli, spinach, onion, garlic, nutmeg, olive oil, and salt in a medium bowl, tossing to coat. Arrange the broccoli in a single layer in the parchment-lined frying basket and cook for 5 minutes. Remove and set to the side.

2. Use the same medium bowl to whisk eggs, salt, pepper, scallions, and sour cream. Add the roasted broccoli and ¼ cup fontina cheese until all ingredients are well combined. Pour the mixture into a greased baking dish and top with cheese. Bake in the air fryer for 15-18 minutes until the center is set. Serve and enjoy.

Apple & Turkey Breakfast Sausages

Servings: 4

Cooking Time: 15 Minutes

Ingredients:

- ½ tsp coriander seeds, crushed
- 1 tbsp chopped rosemary
- 1 tbsp chopped thyme
- Salt and pepper to taste
- 1 tsp fennel seeds, crushed
- ¾ tsp smoked paprika
- ½ tsp garlic powder
- ½ tsp shallot powder
- ⅛ tsp red pepper flakes
- 1 pound ground turkey
- ½ cup minced apples

Directions:

1. Combine all of the seasonings in a bowl. Add turkey and apple and blend seasonings in well with your hands. Form patties about 3 inches in diameter and ¼ inch thick.

2. Preheat air fryer to 400°F. Arrange patties in a single layer on the greased frying basket. Air Fry for 10 minutes, flipping once until brown and cooked through. Serve.

Chapter 2 Poultry Recipes

Spinach And Feta Stuffed Chicken Breasts

Servings: 4

Cooking Time: 27 Minutes

Ingredients:

- 1 (10-ounce) package frozen spinach, thawed and drained well
- 1 cup feta cheese, crumbled
- ½ teaspoon freshly ground black pepper
- 4 boneless chicken breasts
- salt and freshly ground black pepper
- 1 tablespoon olive oil

Directions:

1. Prepare the filling. Squeeze out as much liquid as possible from the thawed spinach. Rough chop the spinach and transfer it to a mixing bowl with the feta cheese and the freshly ground black pepper.

2. Prepare the chicken breast. Place the chicken breast on a cutting board and press down on the chicken breast with one hand to keep it stabilized. Make an incision about 1-inch long in the fattest side of the breast. Move the knife up and down inside the chicken breast, without poking through either the top or the bottom, or the other side of the breast. The inside pocket should be about 3-inches long, but the opening should only be about 1-inch wide. If this is too difficult, you can make the incision longer, but you will have to be more careful when cooking the chicken breast since this will expose more of the stuffing.

3. Once you have prepared the chicken breasts, use your fingers to stuff the filling into each pocket, spreading the mixture down as far as you can.

4. Preheat the air fryer to 380°F.

5. Lightly brush or spray the air fryer basket and the chicken breasts with olive oil. Transfer two of the stuffed chicken breasts to the air fryer. Air-fry for 12 minutes, turning the chicken breasts over halfway through the cooking time. Remove the chicken to a resting plate and air-fry the second two breasts for 12 minutes. Return the first batch of chicken to the air fryer with the second batch and air-fry for 3 more minutes. When the chicken is cooked, an instant read thermometer should register 165°F in the thickest part of the chicken, as well as in the stuffing.

6. Remove the chicken breasts and let them rest on a cutting board for 2 to 3 minutes. Slice the chicken on the bias and serve with the slices fanned out.

Chicken Pigs In Blankets

Servings: 4

Cooking Time: 40 Minutes

Ingredients:

- 8 chicken drumsticks, boneless, skinless
- 2 tbsp light brown sugar
- 2 tbsp ketchup
- 1 tbsp grainy mustard
- 8 smoked bacon slices
- 1 tsp chopped fresh sage

Directions:

1. Preheat the air fryer to 350°F. Mix brown sugar, sage, ketchup, and mustard in a bowl and brush the chicken with it. Wrap slices of bacon around the drumsticks and brush with the remaining mix. Line the frying basket with round parchment paper with holes. Set 4 drumsticks on the paper, add a raised rack and set the other drumsticks on it. Bake for 25-35 minutes, moving the bottom drumsticks to the top, top to the bottom, and flipping at about 14-16 minutes. Sprinkle with sage and serve.

Spinach & Turkey Meatballs

Servings: 4

Cooking Time: 45 Minutes

Ingredients:

- ¼ cup grated Parmesan cheese
- 2 scallions, chopped
- 1 garlic clove, minced
- 1 egg, beaten
- 1 cup baby spinach
- ¼ cup bread crumbs
- 1 tsp dried oregano
- Salt and pepper to taste
- 1 ¼ lb ground turkey

Directions:

1. Preheat the air fryer to 400°F and preheat the oven to 250°F. Combine the scallions, garlic, egg, baby spinach, breadcrumbs, Parmesan, oregano, salt, and pepper in a bowl and mix well. Add the turkey and mix, then form into 1½-inch balls. Add as many meatballs as will fit in a single layer in the frying basket and Air Fry for 10-15 minutes, shaking once around minute 7. Put the cooked meatballs on a tray in the oven and cover with foil to keep warm. Repeat with the remaining balls.

Chicken Adobo

Servings: 6

Cooking Time: 12 Minutes

Ingredients:

- 6 boneless chicken thighs
- ¼ cup soy sauce or tamari
- ½ cup rice wine vinegar
- 4 cloves garlic, minced
- ⅛ teaspoon crushed red pepper flakes
- ½ teaspoon black pepper

Directions:

1. Place the chicken thighs into a resealable plastic bag with the soy sauce or tamari, the rice wine vinegar, the garlic, and the crushed red pepper flakes. Seal the bag and let the chicken marinate at least 1 hour in the refrigerator.

2. Preheat the air fryer to 400°F.

3. Drain the chicken and pat dry with a paper towel. Season the chicken with black pepper and liberally spray with cooking spray.

4. Place the chicken in the air fryer basket and cook for 9 minutes, turn over at 9 minutes and check for an internal temperature of 165°F, and cook another 3 minutes.

Pulled Turkey Quesadillas

Servings: 4

Cooking Time: 15 Minutes

Ingredients:

- ¾ cup pulled cooked turkey breast
- 6 tortilla wraps
- 1/3 cup grated Swiss cheese
- 1 small red onion, sliced
- 2 tbsp Mexican chili sauce

Directions:

1. Preheat air fryer to 400°F. Lay 3 tortilla wraps on a clean workspace, then spoon equal amounts of Swiss cheese, turkey, Mexican chili sauce, and red onion on the tortillas. Spritz the exterior of the tortillas with cooking spray. Air Fry the quesadillas, one at a time, for 5-8 minutes. The cheese should be melted and the outsides crispy. Serve.

Christmas Chicken & Roasted Grape Salad

Servings: 4

Cooking Time: 40 Minutes

Ingredients:

- 3 chicken breasts, pat-dried
- 1 tsp paprika
- Salt and pepper to taste
- 2 cups seedless red grapes
- ½ cup mayonnaise
- ½ cup plain yogurt
- 2 tbsp honey mustard
- 2 tbsp fresh lemon juice
- 1 cup chopped celery
- 2 scallions, chopped
- 2 tbsp walnuts, chopped

Directions:

1. Preheat the air fryer to 370°F. Sprinkle the chicken breasts with paprika, salt, and pepper. Transfer to the greased frying basket and Air Fry for 16-19 minutes, flipping once. Remove and set on a cutting board. Put the grapes in the fryer and spray with cooking oil. Fry for 4 minutes or until the grapes are hot and tender.Mix the mayonnaise, yogurt, honey mustard, and lemon juice in a bowl and whisk. Cube the chicken and add to the dressing along with the grapes, walnuts, celery, and scallions. Toss gently and serve.

Buttered Chicken Thighs

Servings: 4

Cooking Time: 30 Minutes

Ingredients:

- 4 bone-in chicken thighs, skinless
- 2 tbsp butter, melted
- 1 tsp garlic powder
- 1 tsp lemon zest
- Salt and pepper to taste
- 1 lemon, sliced

Directions:

1. Preheat air fryer to 380°F.Stir the chicken thighs in the butter, lemon zest, garlic powder, and salt. Divide the chicken thighs between 4 pieces of foil and sprinkle with black pepper, and then top with slices of lemon. Bake in the air fryer for 20-22 minutes until golden. Serve.

Sticky Drumsticks

Servings: 4

Cooking Time: 45 Minutes

Ingredients:

- 1 lb chicken drumsticks
- 1 tbsp chicken seasoning
- 1 tsp dried chili flakes
- Salt and pepper to taste
- ¼ cup honey
- 1 cup barbecue sauce

Directions:

1. Preheat air fryer to 390°F. Season drumsticks with chicken seasoning, chili flakes, salt, and pepper. Place one batch of drumsticks in the greased frying basket and Air Fry for 18-20 minutes, flipping once until golden.

2. While the chicken is cooking, combine honey and barbecue sauce in a small bowl. Remove the drumsticks to a serving dish. Drizzle honey-barbecue sauce over and serve.

Boss Chicken Cobb Salad

Servings: 2

Cooking Time: 30 Minutes

Ingredients:

- 4 oz cooked bacon, crumbled
- ¼ cup diced peeled red onion
- ½ cup crumbled blue cheese
- 1 egg
- 1 tbsp honey
- 1 tbsp Dijon mustard
- ½ tsp apple cider vinegar
- 2 chicken breasts, cubed
- 3/4 cup bread crumbs
- Salt and pepper to taste
- 3 cups torn iceberg lettuce
- 2 cups baby spinach
- ½ cup ranch dressing
- ½ avocado, diced
- 1 beefsteak tomato, diced
- 1 hard-boiled egg, diced
- 2 tbsp parsley

Directions:

1. Preheat air fryer at 350ºF. Mix the egg, honey, mustard, and vinegar in a bowl. Toss in chicken cubes to coat. Shake off excess marinade of chicken. In another bowl, combine breadcrumbs, salt, and pepper. Dredge chicken cubes in the mixture. Place chicken cubes in the greased frying basket. Air Fry for 8-10 minutes, tossing once. In a salad bowl, combine lettuce, baby spinach, and ranch dressing and toss to coat. Add in the cooked chicken and the remaining ingredients. Serve immediately.

Gruyère Asparagus & Chicken Quiche

Servings: 4

Cooking Time: 30 Minutes

Ingredients:

- 1 grilled chicken breasts, diced
- ½ cup shredded Gruyère cheese
- 1 premade pie crust
- 2 eggs, beaten
- ¼ cup milk
- Salt and pepper to taste
- ½ lb asparagus, sliced
- 1 lemon, zested

Directions:

1. Preheat air fryer to 360°F. Carefully press the crust into a baking dish, trimming the edges. Prick the dough with a fork a few times. Add the eggs, milk, asparagus, salt, pepper, chicken, lemon zest, and half of Gruyère cheese to a mixing bowl and stir until completely blended. Pour the mixture into the pie crust. Bake in the air fryer for 15 minutes. Sprinkle the remaining Gruyère cheese on top of the quiche filling. Bake for 5 more minutes until the quiche is golden brown. Remove and allow to cool for a few minutes before cutting. Serve sliced and enjoy!

Turkey Burgers

Servings: 4

Cooking Time: 13 Minutes

Ingredients:

- 1 pound ground turkey
- ¼ cup diced red onion
- 1 tablespoon grilled chicken seasoning
- ½ teaspoon dried parsley
- ½ teaspoon salt
- 4 slices provolone cheese
- 4 whole-grain sandwich buns
- Suggested toppings: lettuce, sliced tomatoes, dill pickles, and mustard

Directions:

1. Combine the turkey, onion, chicken seasoning, parsley, and salt and mix well.
2. Shape into 4 patties.
3. Cook at 360°F for 11 minutes or until turkey is well done and juices run clear.
4. Top each burger with a slice of cheese and cook 2 minutes to melt.
5. Serve on buns with your favorite toppings.

Asian Meatball Tacos

Servings: 4

Cooking Time: 10 Minutes

Ingredients:

- 1 pound lean ground turkey
- 3 tablespoons soy sauce
- 1 tablespoon brown sugar
- ½ teaspoon onion powder
- ½ teaspoon garlic powder
- 1 tablespoon sesame seeds
- 1 English cucumber
- 4 radishes
- 2 tablespoons white wine vinegar
- 1 lime, juiced and divided
- 1 tablespoon avocado oil
- Salt, to taste
- ½ cup Greek yogurt
- 1 to 3 teaspoons Sriracha, based on desired spiciness
- 1 cup shredded cabbage
- ¼ cup chopped cilantro
- Eight 6-inch flour tortillas

Directions:

1. Preheat the air fryer to 360°F.
2. In a large bowl, mix the ground turkey, soy sauce, brown sugar, onion powder, garlic powder, and sesame seeds. Form the meat into 1-inch meatballs and place in the air fryer basket. Cook for 5 minutes, shake the basket, and cook another 5 minutes. Using a food thermometer, make sure the internal temperature of the meatballs is 165°F.
3. Meanwhile, dice the cucumber and radishes and place in a medium bowl. Add the white wine vinegar, 1 teaspoon of the lime juice, and the avocado oil, and stir to coat. Season with salt to desired taste.
4. In a large bowl, mix the Greek yogurt, Sriracha, and the remaining lime juice, and stir. Add in the cabbage and cilantro; toss well to create a slaw.
5. In a heavy skillet, heat the tortillas over medium heat for 1 to 2 minutes on each side, or until warmed.
6. To serve, place a tortilla on a plate, top with 5 meatballs, then with cucumber and radish salad, and finish with 2 tablespoons of cabbage slaw.

Basic Chicken Breasts(1)

Servings: 4
Cooking Time: 15 Minutes
Ingredients:

- 2 tsp olive oil
- 4 chicken breasts
- Salt and pepper to taste
- 1 tbsp Italian seasoning

Directions:

1. Preheat air fryer at 350ºF. Rub olive oil over chicken breasts and sprinkle with salt, Italian seasoning and black pepper. Place them in the frying basket and Air Fry for 8-10 minutes. Let rest for 5 minutes before cutting. Store it covered in the fridge for up to 1 week.

Greek Chicken Wings

Servings: 4
Cooking Time: 30 Minutes
Ingredients:

- 8 whole chicken wings
- ½ lemon, juiced
- ½ tsp garlic powder
- 1 tsp shallot powder
- ½ tsp Greek seasoning
- Salt and pepper to taste
- ¼ cup buttermilk
- ½ cup all-purpose flour

Directions:

1. Preheat air fryer to 400°F. Put the wings in a resealable bag along with lemon juice, garlic, shallot, Greek seasoning, salt and pepper. Seal the bag and shake to coat. Set up bowls large enough to fit the wings.
2. In one bowl, pour the buttermilk. In the other, add flour. Using tongs, dip the wings into the buttermilk, then dredge in flour. Transfer the wings in the greased frying basket, spraying lightly with cooking oil. Air Fry for 25 minutes, shaking twice, until golden and cooked through. Allow to cool slightly, and serve.

Turkey Steaks With Green Salad

Servings: 4

Cooking Time: 20 Minutes

Ingredients:

- 1/3 cup shaved Parmesan cheese
- 3 tsp grated Parmesan cheese
- 4 turkey breast steaks
- Salt and pepper to taste
- 1 large egg, beaten
- ½ cup bread crumbs
- ½ tsp dried thyme
- 5 oz baby spinach
- 5 oz watercress
- 1 tbsp olive oil
- 1 tbsp lemon juice
- 2 spring onions, chopped
- 1 lemon, cut into wedges

Directions:

1.   Place the steaks between two sheets of parchment paper. Pound the turkey to ¼-inch thick cutlets using a meat mallet or rolling pin. Season the cutlets with salt and pepper to taste. Put the beaten egg in a shallow bowl. Put the crumbs, thyme, and Parmesan in a second shallow bowl. Dip the cutlet in the egg bowl and then in the crumb mix. Press the crumbs so that they stick to the chicken. Preheat air fryer to 400°F. Fry the turkey in the greased frying basket for 8 minutes, flipping once until golden and cooked through. Repeat for all cutlets.

2.   Put the spinach, spring onions, and watercress in a bowl. Toss with olive oil, lemon juice, salt, and pepper. Serve each cutlet on a plate topped with 1 ½ cups salad. Garnish with lemon wedges and shaved Parmesan cheese. Serve.

Easy Turkey Meatballs

Servings: 4

Cooking Time: 20 Minutes

Ingredients:

- 1 lb ground turkey
- ½ celery stalk, chopped
- 1 egg
- ¼ tsp red pepper flakes
- ¼ cup bread crumbs
- Salt and pepper to taste
- ½ tsp garlic powder
- ½ tsp onion powder
- ½ tsp cayenne pepper

Directions:

1.   Preheat air fryer to 360°F. Add all of the ingredients to a bowl and mix well. Shape the mixture into 12 balls and arrange them on the greased frying basket. Air Fry for 10-12 minutes or until the meatballs are cooked through and browned. Serve and enjoy!

Masala Chicken With Charred Vegetables

Servings: 4
Cooking Time: 35 Minutes
Ingredients:

- 8 boneless, skinless chicken thighs
- ¼ cup yogurt
- 3 garlic cloves, minced
- 1 tbsp lime juice
- 1 tsp ginger-garlic paste
- 1 tsp garam masala
- ¼ tsp ground turmeric
- ¼ tsp red pepper flakes
- 1 ¼ tsp salt
- 7 oz shishito peppers
- 2 vine tomatoes, quartered
- 1 tbsp chopped cilantro
- 1 lime, cut into wedges

Directions:

1. Mix yogurt, garlic, lime juice, ginger paste, garam masala, turmeric, flakes, and salt in a bowl. Place the thighs in a zipper bag and pour in the marinade. Massage the chicken to coat and refrigerate for 2 hours.

2. Preheat air fryer to 400°F. Remove the chicken from the bag and discard the marinade. Put the chicken in the greased frying basket and Arr Fry for 13-15 minutes, flipping once until browned and thoroughly cooked. Set chicken aside and cover with foil. Lightly spray shishitos and tomatoes with cooking oil. Place in the frying basket and Bake for 8 minutes, shaking the basket once until soft and slightly charred. Sprinkle with salt. Top the chicken and veggies with cilantro and lemon wedges.

Moroccan-style Chicken Strips

Servings: 4
Cooking Time: 30 Minutes
Ingredients:

- 4 chicken breasts, cut into strips
- 2 tsp olive oil
- 2 tbsp cornstarch
- 3 garlic cloves, minced
- ½ cup chicken broth
- ¼ cup lemon juice
- 1 tbsp honey
- ½ tsp ras el hanout
- 1 cup cooked couscous

Directions:

1. Preheat air fryer to 400°F. Mix the chicken and olive oil in a bowl, then add the cornstarch. Stir to coat. Add the garlic and transfer to a baking pan. Put the pan in the fryer. Bake for 10 minutes. Stir at least once during cooking.

2. When done, pour in the chicken broth, lemon juice, honey, and ras el hanout. Bake for an additional 6-9 minutes or until the sauce is thick and the chicken cooked through with no pink showing. Serve with couscous.

Cajun Fried Chicken

Servings: 3

Cooking Time: 35 Minutes

Ingredients:

- 1 cup Cajun seasoning
- ½ tsp mango powder
- 6 chicken legs, bone-in

Directions:

1. Preheat air fryer to 360°F. Place half of the Cajun seasoning and 3/4 cup of water in a bowl and mix well to dissolve any lumps. Add the remaining Cajun seasoning and mango powder to a shallow bowl and stir to combine. Dip the chicken in the batter, then coat it in the mango seasoning. Lightly spritz the chicken with cooking spray. Place the chicken in the air fryer and Air Fry for 14-16 minutes, turning once until the chicken is cooked and the coating is brown. Serve and enjoy!

German Chicken Frikadellen

Servings: 6

Cooking Time: 20 Minutes

Ingredients:

- 1 lb ground chicken
- 1 egg
- 3/4 cup bread crumbs
- ¼ cup diced onions
- 1 grated carrot
- 1 tsp yellow mustard
- Salt and pepper to taste
- ¼ cup chopped parsley

Directions:

1. Preheat air fryer at 350ºF. In a bowl, combine the ground chicken, egg, crumbs, onions, carrot, parsley, salt, and pepper. Mix well with your hands. Form mixture into meatballs. Place them in the frying basket and Air Fry for 8-10 minutes, tossing once until golden. Serve right away.

Chapter 3 Beef ，pork & Lamb Recipes

Extra Crispy Country-style Pork Riblets

Servings: 3
Cooking Time: 30 Minutes
Ingredients:

- ⅓ cup Tapioca flour
- 2½ tablespoons Chile powder
- ¾ teaspoon Table salt (optional)
- 1¼ pounds Boneless country-style pork ribs, cut into 1½-inch chunks
- Vegetable oil spray

Directions:

1. Preheat the air fryer to 375°F .
2. Mix the tapioca flour, chile powder, and salt (if using) in a large bowl until well combined. Add the country-style rib chunks and toss well to coat thoroughly.
3. When the machine is at temperature, gently shake off any excess tapioca coating from the chunks. Generously coat them on all sides with vegetable oil spray. Arrange the chunks in the basket in one (admittedly fairly tight) layer. The pieces may touch. Air-fry for 30 minutes, rearranging the pieces at the 10- and 20-minute marks to expose any touching bits, until very crisp and well browned.
4. Gently pour the contents of the basket onto a wire rack. Cool for 5 minutes before serving.

Pork Schnitzel

Servings: 4
Cooking Time: 14 Minutes
Ingredients:

- 4 boneless pork chops, pounded to ¼-inch thickness
- 1 teaspoon salt, divided
- 1 teaspoon black pepper, divided
- ½ cup all-purpose flour
- 2 eggs
- 1 cup breadcrumbs
- ¼ teaspoon paprika
- 1 lemon, cut into wedges

Directions:

1. Season both sides of the pork chops with ½ teaspoon of the salt and ½ teaspoon of the pepper.
2. On a plate, place the flour.
3. In a large bowl, whisk the eggs.
4. In another large bowl, place the breadcrumbs.
5. Season the flour with the paprika and season the breadcrumbs with the remaining ½ teaspoon of salt and ½ teaspoon of pepper.
6. To bread the pork, place a pork chop in the flour, then into the whisked eggs, and then into the breadcrumbs. Place the breaded pork onto a plate and finish breading the remaining pork chops.
7. Preheat the air fryer to 390°F.
8. Place the pork chops into the air fryer, not overlapping and working in batches as needed. Spray the pork chops with cooking spray and cook for 8 minutes; flip the pork and cook for another 4 to 6 minutes or until cooked to an internal temperature of 145°F.
9. Serve with lemon wedges.

Paprika Fried Beef

Servings: 4

Cooking Time: 30 Minutes

Ingredients:

- Celery salt to taste
- 4 beef cube steaks
- ½ cup milk
- 1 cup flour
- 2 tsp paprika
- 1 egg
- 1 cup bread crumbs
- 2 tbsp olive oil

Directions:

1. Preheat air fryer to 350°F. Place the cube steaks in a zipper sealed bag or between two sheets of cling wrap. Gently pound the steaks until they are slightly thinner. Set aside. In a bowl, mix together milk, flour, paprika, celery salt, and egg until just combined. In a separate bowl, mix together the crumbs and olive oil. Take the steaks and dip them into the buttermilk batter, shake off some of the excess, and return to a plate for 5 minutes. Next, dip the steaks in the bread crumbs, patting the crumbs into both sides. Air Fry the steaks until the crust is crispy and brown, 12-16 minutes. Serve warm.

Vietnamese Shaking Beef

Servings: 3

Cooking Time: 7 Minutes

Ingredients:

- 1 pound Beef tenderloin, cut into 1-inch cubes
- 1 tablespoon Regular or low-sodium soy sauce or gluten-free tamari sauce
- 1 tablespoon Fish sauce (gluten-free, if a concern)
- 1 tablespoon Dark brown sugar
- 1½ teaspoons Ground black pepper
- 3 Medium scallions, trimmed and thinly sliced
- 2 tablespoons Butter
- 1½ teaspoons Minced garlic

Directions:

1. Mix the beef, soy or tamari sauce, fish sauce, and brown sugar in a bowl until well combined. Cover and refrigerate for at least 2 hours or up to 8 hours, tossing the beef at least twice in the marinade.

2. Put a 6-inch round or square cake pan in an air-fryer basket for a small batch, a 7-inch round or square cake pan for a medium batch, or an 8-inch round or square cake pan for a large one. Or put one of these on the rack of a toaster oven–style air fryer. Heat the machine with the pan in it to 400°F. When the machine it at temperature, let the pan sit in the heat for 2 to 3 minutes so that it gets very hot.

3. Use a slotted spoon to transfer the beef to the pan, leaving any marinade behind in the bowl. Spread the meat into as close to an even layer as you can. Air-fry undisturbed for 5 minutes. Meanwhile, discard the marinade, if any.

4. Add the scallions, butter, and garlic to the beef. Air-fry for 2 minutes, tossing and rearranging the beef and scallions repeatedly, perhaps every 20 seconds.

5. Remove the basket from the machine and let the meat cool in the pan for a couple of minutes before serving.

Garlic-buttered Rib Eye Steak

Servings: 2
Cooking Time: 25 Minutes
Ingredients:

- 1 lb rib eye steak
- Salt and pepper to taste
- 1 tbsp butter
- 1 tsp paprika
- 1 tbsp chopped rosemary
- 2 garlic cloves, minced
- 2 tbsp chopped parsley
- 1 tbsp chopped mint

Directions:

1. Preheat air fryer to 400°F. Sprinkle salt and pepper on both sides of the rib eye. Transfer the rib eye to the greased frying basket, then top with butter, mint, paprika, rosemary, and garlic. Bake for 6 minutes, then flip the steak. Bake for another 6 minutes. For medium-rare, the steak needs to reach an internal temperature of 140°F. Allow resting for 5 minutes before slicing. Serve sprinkled with parsley and enjoy!

Country-style Pork Ribs(2)

Servings:4
Cooking Time: 50 Minutes
Ingredients:

- 1 tsp smoked paprika
- 1 tsp ground cumin
- 1 tsp garlic powder
- 1 tsp onion powder
- 1 tbsp honey
- ½ tsp ground mustard
- Salt and pepper to taste
- 2 tbsp olive oil
- 1 tbsp fresh orange juice
- 2 lb country-style pork ribs

Directions:

1. Preheat air fryer to 350ºF. Combine all spices and honey in a bowl. In another bowl, whisk olive oil and orange juice and massage onto pork ribs. Sprinkle with the spice mixture. Place the pork ribs in the frying basket and Air Fry for 40 minutes, flipping every 10 minutes. Serve.

Crispy Five-spice Pork Belly

Servings: 6

Cooking Time: 60-75 Minutes

Ingredients:

- 1½ pounds Pork belly with skin
- 3 tablespoons Shaoxing (Chinese cooking rice wine), dry sherry, or white grape juice
- 1½ teaspoons Granulated white sugar
- ¾ teaspoon Five-spice powder (see the headnote)
- 1¼ cups Coarse sea salt or kosher salt

Directions:

1. Preheat the air fryer to 350°F .

2. Set the pork belly skin side up on a cutting board. Use a meat fork to make dozens and dozens of tiny holes all across the surface of the skin. You can hardly make too many holes. These will allow the skin to bubble up and keep it from becoming hard as it roasts.

3. Turn the pork belly over so that one of its longer sides faces you. Make four evenly spaced vertical slits in the meat. The slits should go about halfway into the meat toward the fat.

4. Mix the Shaoxing or its substitute, sugar, and five-spice powder in a small bowl until the sugar dissolves. Massage this mixture across the meat and into the cuts.

5. Turn the pork belly over again. Blot dry any moisture on the skin. Make a double-thickness aluminum foil tray by setting two 10-inch-long pieces of foil on top of another. Set the pork belly skin side up in the center of this tray. Fold the sides of the tray up toward the pork, crimping the foil as you work to make a high-sided case all around the pork belly. Seal the foil to the meat on all sides so that only the skin is exposed.

6. Pour the salt onto the skin and pat it down and in place to create a crust. Pick up the foil tray with the pork in it and set it in the basket.

7. Air-fry undisturbed for 35 minutes for a small batch, 45 minutes for a medium batch, or 50 minutes for a large batch.

8. Remove the foil tray with the pork belly still in it. Warning: The foil tray is full of scalding-hot fat. Discard the fat in the tray (not down the drain!), as well as the tray itself. Transfer the pork belly to a cutting board.

9. Raise the air fryer temperature to 375°F (or 380°F or 390°F, if one of these is the closest setting). Brush the salt crust off the pork, removing any visible salt from the sides of the meat, too.

10. When the machine is at temperature, return the pork belly skin side up to the basket. Air-fry undisturbed for 25 minutes, or until crisp and very well browned. If the machine is at 390°F, you may be able to shave 5 minutes off the cooking time so that the skin doesn't blacken.

11. Use a nonstick-safe spatula, and perhaps a silicone baking mitt, to transfer the pork belly to a wire rack. Cool for 10 minutes before serving.

Barbecue-style Beef Cube Steak

Servings: 2
Cooking Time: 14 Minutes
Ingredients:

- 2 4-ounce beef cube steak(s)
- 2 cups (about 8 ounces) Fritos (original flavor) or a generic corn chip equivalent, crushed to crumbs (see here)
- 6 tablespoons Purchased smooth barbecue sauce, any flavor (gluten-free, if a concern)

Directions:

1. Preheat the air fryer to 375°F .
2. Spread the Fritos crumbs in a shallow soup plate or a small pie plate. Rub the barbecue sauce onto both sides of the steak(s). Dredge the steak(s) in the Fritos crumbs to coat well and thoroughly, turning several times and pressing down to get the little bits to adhere to the meat.
3. When the machine is at temperature, set the steak(s) in the basket. Leave as much air space between them as possible if you're working with more than one piece of beef. Air-fry undisturbed for 12 minutes, or until lightly brown and crunchy. If the machine is at 360°F, you may need to add 2 minutes to the cooking time.
4. Use kitchen tongs to transfer the steak(s) to a wire rack. Cool for 5 minutes before serving.

Tuscan Chimichangas

Servings: 2
Cooking Time: 8 Minutes
Ingredients:

- ¼ pound Thinly sliced deli ham, chopped
- 1 cup Drained and rinsed canned white beans
- ½ cup (about 2 ounces) Shredded semi-firm mozzarella
- ¼ cup Chopped sun-dried tomatoes
- ¼ cup Bottled Italian salad dressing, vinaigrette type
- 2 Burrito-size (12-inch) flour tortilla(s)
- Olive oil spray

Directions:

1. Preheat the air fryer to 375°F .
2. Mix the ham, beans, cheese, tomatoes, and salad dressing in a bowl.
3. Lay a tortilla on a clean, dry work surface. Put all of the ham mixture in a narrow oval in the middle of the tortilla, if making one burrito; or half of this mixture, if making two. Fold the parts of the tortilla that are closest to the ends of the filling oval up and over the filling, then roll the tortilla tightly closed, but don't press down hard. Generously coat the tortilla with olive oil spray. Make a second filled tortilla, if necessary.
4. Set the filled tortilla(s) seam side down in the basket, with at least ½ inch between them, if making two. Air-fry undisturbed for 8 minutes, or until crisp and lightly browned.
5. Use kitchen tongs and a nonstick-safe spatula to transfer the chimichanga(s) to a wire rack. Cool for 5 minutes before serving.

Cal-mex Chimichangas

Servings: 4
Cooking Time: 30 Minutes
Ingredients:

- 1 can diced tomatoes with chiles
- 1 cup shredded cheddar
- ½ cup chopped onions
- 2 garlic cloves, minced
- 1 lb ground beef
- 2 tbsp taco seasoning
- Salt and pepper to taste
- 4 flour tortillas
- ½ cup Pico de Gallo

Directions:

1. Warm the olive oil in a skillet over medium heat and stir-fry the onion and garlic for 3 minutes or until fragrant. Add ground beef, taco seasoning, salt and pepper. Stir and break up the beef with a spoon. Cook for 3-4 minutes or until it is browned. Stir in diced tomatoes with chiles. Scoop ½ cup of beef onto each tortilla. Form chimichangas by folding the sides of the tortilla into the middle, then roll up from the bottom. Use a toothpick to secure the chimichanga.

2. Preheat air fryer to 400°F. Lightly spray the chimichangas with cooking oil. Place the first batch in the fryer and Bake for 8 minutes. Transfer to a serving dish and top with shredded cheese and pico de gallo.

Corned Beef Hash

Servings: 6
Cooking Time: 15 Minutes
Ingredients:

- 3 cups (about 14 ounces) Frozen unseasoned hash brown cubes (no need to thaw)
- 9 ounces Deli corned beef, cut into ¾-inch-thick slices, then cubed
- ¾ cup Roughly chopped yellow or white onion
- ¾ cup Stemmed, cored, and roughly chopped red bell pepper
- 2½ tablespoons Olive oil
- ¼ teaspoon Dried thyme
- ¼ teaspoon Dried sage leaves
- Up to a ⅛ teaspoon Cayenne

Directions:

1. Preheat the air fryer to 400°F.

2. Mix all the ingredients in a large or very large bowl until the potato cubes and corned beef are coated in the spices.

3. Spread the mixture in the basket in as close to an even layer as you can. Air-fry for 15 minutes, tossing and rearranging the pieces at the 5- and 10-minute marks to expose covered bits, until the potatoes are browned, even crisp, and the mixture is very fragrant.

4. Pour the contents of the basket onto a serving platter or divide between serving plates. Cool for a couple of minutes before serving.

Carne Asada

Servings: 4

Cooking Time: 15 Minutes

Ingredients:

- 4 cloves garlic, minced
- 3 chipotle peppers in adobo, chopped
- ⅓ cup chopped fresh parsley
- ⅓ cup chopped fresh oregano
- 1 teaspoon ground cumin seed
- juice of 2 limes
- ⅓ cup olive oil
- 1 to 1½ pounds flank steak (depending on your appetites)
- salt
- tortillas and guacamole (optional – for serving)

Directions:

1. Make the marinade: Combine the garlic, chipotle, parsley, oregano, cumin, lime juice and olive oil in a non-reactive bowl. Coat the flank steak with the marinade and let it marinate for 30 minutes to 8 hours. (Don't leave the steak out of refrigeration for longer than 2 hours, however.)

2. Preheat the air fryer to 390°F.

3. Remove the steak from the marinade and place it in the air fryer basket. Season the steak with salt and air-fry for 15 minutes, turning the steak over halfway through the cooking time and seasoning again with salt. This should cook the steak to medium. Add or subtract two minutes for medium-well or medium-rare.

4. Remember to let the steak rest before slicing the meat against the grain. Serve with warm tortillas, guacamole and a fresh salsa like the Tomato-Corn Salsa below.

Tender Steak With Salsa Verde

Servings:4

Cooking Time: 20 Minutes

Ingredients:

- 1 flank steak, halved
- 1 ½ cups salsa verde
- ½ tsp black pepper

Directions:

1. Toss steak and 1 cup of salsa verde in a bowl and refrigerate covered for 2 hours. Preheat air fryer to 400ºF.Add steaks to the lightly greased frying basket and Air Fry for 10-12 minutes or until you reach your desired doneness, flipping once. Let sit onto a cutting board for 5 minutes. Thinly slice against the grain and divide between 4 plates. Spoon over the remaining salsa verde and serve sprinkled with black pepper to serve.

Beef Short Ribs

Servings: 4

Cooking Time: 20 Minutes

Ingredients:

- 2 tablespoons soy sauce
- 1 tablespoon sesame oil
- 2 tablespoons brown sugar
- 1 teaspoon ground ginger
- 2 garlic cloves, crushed
- 1 pound beef short ribs

Directions:

1. In a small bowl, mix together the soy sauce, sesame oil, brown sugar, and ginger. Transfer the mixture to a large resealable plastic bag, and place the garlic cloves and short ribs into the bag. Secure and place in the refrigerator for an hour (or overnight).
2. When you're ready to prepare the dish, preheat the air fryer to 330°F.
3. Liberally spray the air fryer basket with olive oil mist and set the beef short ribs in the basket.
4. Cook for 10 minutes, flip the short ribs, and then cook another 10 minutes.
5. Remove the short ribs from the air fryer basket, loosely cover with aluminum foil, and let them rest. The short ribs will continue to cook after they're removed from the basket. Check the internal temperature after 5 minutes to make sure it reached 145°F if you prefer a well-done meat. If it didn't reach 145°F and you would like it to be cooked longer, you can put it back into the air fryer basket at 330°F for another 3 minutes.
6. Remove from the basket and let it rest, covered with aluminum foil, for 5 minutes. Serve immediately.

Pepperoni Bagel Pizzas

Servings: 4

Cooking Time: 20 Minutes

Ingredients:

- 2 bagels, halved horizontally
- 2 cups shredded mozzarella
- ¼ cup grated Parmesan
- 1 cup passata
- 1/3 cup sliced pepperoni
- 2 scallions, chopped
- 2 tbsp minced fresh chives
- 1tsp red chili flakes

Directions:

1. Preheat the air fryer to 375°F. Put the bagel halves, cut side up, in the frying basket. Bake for 2-3 minutes until golden. Remove and top them with passata, pepperoni, scallions, and cheeses. Put the bagels topping-side up to the frying basket and cook for 8-12 more minutes or until the bagels are hot and the cheese has melted and is bubbling. Top with the chives and chili flakes and serve.

Skirt Steak With Horseradish Cream

Servings:2
Cooking Time: 20 Minutes
Ingredients:

- 1 cup heavy cream
- 3 tbsp horseradish sauce
- 1 lemon, zested
- 1 skirt steak, halved
- 2 tbsp olive oil
- Salt and pepper to taste

Directions:

1. Mix together the heavy cream, horseradish sauce, and lemon zest in a small bowl. Let chill in the fridge.
2. Preheat air fryer to 400ºF. Brush steak halves with olive oil and sprinkle with salt and pepper. Place steaks in the frying basket and Air Fry for 10 minutes or until you reach your desired doneness, flipping once. Let sit onto a cutting board for 5 minutes.Thinly slice against the grain and divide between 2 plates. Drizzle with the horseradish sauce over. Serve and enjoy!

Chipotle Pork Meatballs

Servings:4
Cooking Time: 35 Minutes
Ingredients:

- 1 lb ground pork
- 1 egg
- ¼ cup chipotle sauce
- ¼ cup grated celery
- ¼ cup chopped parsley
- ¼ cup chopped cilantro
- ¼ cup flour
- ¼ tsp salt

Directions:

1. Preheat air fryer to 350ºF. In a large bowl, combine the ground pork, egg, chipotle sauce, celery, parsley, cilantro, flour, and salt. Form mixture into 16 meatballs. Place the meatballs in the lightly greased frying basket and Air Fry for 8-10 minutes, flipping once. Serve immediately!

Pork Tenderloin With Apples & Celery

Servings: 4
Cooking Time: 30 Minutes
Ingredients:

- 1 lb pork tenderloin, cut into 4 pieces
- 2 Granny Smith apples, sliced
- 1 tbsp butter, melted
- 2 tsp olive oil
- 3 celery stalks, sliced
- 1 onion, sliced
- 2 tsp dried thyme
- 1/3 cup apple juice

Directions:

1. Preheat air fryer to 400°F. Brush olive oil and butter all over the pork, then toss the pork, apples, celery, onion, thyme, and apple juice in a bowl and mix well. Put the bowl in the air fryer and Roast for 15-19 minutes until the pork is cooked through and the apples and veggies are soft, stirring once during cooking. Serve warm.

Lamb Koftas Meatballs

Servings: 3
Cooking Time: 8 Minutes
Ingredients:

- 1 pound ground lamb
- 1 teaspoon ground cumin
- 1 teaspoon ground coriander
- 2 tablespoons chopped fresh mint
- 1 egg, beaten
- ½ teaspoon salt
- freshly ground black pepper

Directions:

1. Combine all ingredients in a bowl and mix together well. Divide the mixture into 10 portions. Roll each portion into a ball and then by cupping the meatball in your hand, shape it into an oval.
2. Preheat the air fryer to 400°F.
3. Air-fry the koftas for 8 minutes.
4. Serve warm with the cucumber-yogurt dip.

Suwon Pork Meatballs

Servings: 4
Cooking Time: 30 Minutes
Ingredients:

- 1 lb ground pork
- 1 egg
- 1 tsp cumin
- 1 tbsp gochujang
- 1 tsp tamari
- ¼ tsp ground ginger
- ¼ cup bread crumbs
- 1 scallion, sliced
- 4 tbsp plum jam
- 1 tsp toasted sesame seeds

Directions:

1. Preheat air fryer at 350°F. In a bowl, combine all ingredients, except scallion greens, sesame seeds and plum jam. Form mixture into meatballs. Place meatballs in the greased frying basket and Air Fry for 8 minutes, flipping once. Garnish with scallion greens, plum jam and toasted sesame seeds to serve.

Chapter 4 Fish And Seafood Recipes

Sweet Potato–wrapped Shrimp

Servings:3

Cooking Time: 6 Minutes

Ingredients:

- 24 Long spiralized sweet potato strands
- Olive oil spray
- ¼ teaspoon Garlic powder
- ¼ teaspoon Table salt
- Up to a ⅛ teaspoon Cayenne
- 12 Large shrimp (20–25 per pound), peeled and deveined

Directions:

1. Preheat the air fryer to 400°F.

2. Lay the spiralized sweet potato strands on a large swath of paper towels and straighten out the strands to long ropes. Coat them with olive oil spray, then sprinkle them with the garlic powder, salt, and cayenne.

3. Pick up 2 strands and wrap them around the center of a shrimp, with the ends tucked under what now becomes the bottom side of the shrimp. Continue wrapping the remainder of the shrimp.

4. Set the shrimp bottom side down in the basket with as much air space between them as possible. Air-fry undisturbed for 6 minutes, or until the sweet potato strands are crisp and the shrimp are pink and firm.

5. Use kitchen tongs to transfer the shrimp to a wire rack. Cool for only a minute or two before serving.

British Fish & Chips

Servings: 4

Cooking Time: 40 Minutes

Ingredients:

- 2 peeled russet potatoes, thinly sliced
- 1 egg white
- 1 tbsp lemon juice
- 1/3 cup ground almonds
- 2 bread slices, crumbled
- ½ tsp dried basil
- 4 haddock fillets

Directions:

1. Preheat air fryer to 390°F. Lay the potato slices in the frying basket and Air Fry for 11-15 minutes. Turn the fries a couple of times while cooking. While the fries are cooking, whisk the egg white and lemon juice together in a bowl. On a plate, combine the almonds, breadcrumbs, and basil. First, one at a time, dip the fillets into the egg mix and then coat in the almond/breadcrumb mix. Lay the fillets on a wire rack until the fries are done. Preheat the oven to 350°F. After the fries are done, move them to a pan and place in the oven to keep warm. Put the fish in the frying basket and Air Fry for 10-14 minutes or until cooked through, golden, and crispy. Serve with the fries.

Mojito Fish Tacos

Servings: 4
Cooking Time: 30 Minutes

Ingredients:

- 1 ½ cups chopped red cabbage
- 1 lb cod fillets
- 2 tsp olive oil
- 3 tbsp lemon juice
- 1 large carrot, grated
- 1 tbsp white rum
- ½ cup salsa
- 1/3 cup Greek yogurt
- 4 soft tortillas

Directions:

1. Preheat air fryer to 390°F. Rub the fish with olive oil, then a splash with a tablespoon of lemon juice. Place in the fryer and Air Fry for 9-12 minutes. The fish should flake when done. Mix the remaining lemon juice, red cabbage, carrots, salsa, rum, and yogurt in a bowl. Take the fish out of the fryer and tear into large pieces. Serve with tortillas and cabbage mixture. Enjoy!

Salmon Puttanesca En Papillotte With Zucchini

Servings: 2
Cooking Time: 17 Minutes

Ingredients:

- 1 small zucchini, sliced into ¼-inch thick half moons
- 1 teaspoon olive oil
- salt and freshly ground black pepper
- 2 (5-ounce) salmon fillets
- 1 beefsteak tomato, chopped (about 1 cup)
- 1 tablespoon capers, rinsed
- 10 black olives, pitted and sliced
- 2 tablespoons dry vermouth or white wine 2 tablespoons butter
- ¼ cup chopped fresh basil, chopped

Directions:

1. Preheat the air fryer to 400°F.

2. Toss the zucchini with the olive oil, salt and freshly ground black pepper. Transfer the zucchini into the air fryer basket and air-fry for 5 minutes, shaking the basket once or twice during the cooking process.

3. Cut out 2 large rectangles of parchment paper – about 13-inches by 15-inches each. Divide the air-fried zucchini between the two pieces of parchment paper, placing the vegetables in the center of each rectangle.

4. Place a fillet of salmon on each pile of zucchini. Season the fish very well with salt and pepper. Toss the tomato, capers, olives and vermouth (or white wine) together in a bowl. Divide the tomato mixture between the two fish packages, placing it on top of the fish fillets and pouring any juice out of the bowl onto the fish. Top each fillet with a tablespoon of butter.

5. Fold up each parchment square. Bring two edges together and fold them over a few times, leaving some space above the fish. Twist the open sides together and upwards so they can serve as handles for the packet, but don't let them extend beyond the top of the air fryer basket.

6. Place the two packages into the air fryer and air-fry at 400°F for 12 minutes. The packages should be puffed up and slightly browned when fully cooked. Once cooked, let the fish sit in the parchment for 2 minutes.

7. Serve the fish in the parchment paper, or if desired, remove the parchment paper before serving. Garnish with a little fresh basil.

Spiced Salmon Croquettes

Servings: 6
Cooking Time: 20 Minutes
Ingredients:

- 1 can Alaskan pink salmon, bones removed
- 1 lime, zested
- 1 red chili, minced
- 2 tbsp cilantro, chopped
- 1 egg, beaten
- ½ cup bread crumbs
- 2 scallions, diced
- 1 tsp garlic powder
- Salt and pepper to taste

Directions:

1. Preheat air fryer to 400°F. Mix salmon, beaten egg, bread crumbs and scallions in a large bowl. Add garlic, lime, red chili, cilantro, salt and pepper. Divide into 6 even portions and shape into patties. Place them in the greased frying basket and Air Fry for 7 minutes. Flip them and cook for 4 minutes or until golden. Serve.

Chili Blackened Shrimp

Servings: 4
Cooking Time: 15 Minutes
Ingredients:

- 1 lb peeled shrimp, deveined
- 1 tsp paprika
- ½ tsp dried dill
- ½ tsp red chili flakes
- ½ lemon, juiced
- Salt and pepper to taste

Directions:

1. Preheat air fryer to 400°F. In a resealable bag, add shrimp, paprika, dill, red chili flakes, lemon juice, salt and pepper. Seal and shake well. Place the shrimp in the greased frying basket and Air Fry for 7-8 minutes, shaking the basket once until blackened. Let cool slightly and serve.

Beer-battered Cod

Servings:3

Cooking Time: 12 Minutes

Ingredients:

- 1½ cups All-purpose flour
- 3 tablespoons Old Bay seasoning
- 1 Large egg(s)
- ¼ cup Amber beer, pale ale, or IPA
- 3 4-ounce skinless cod fillets
- Vegetable oil spray

Directions:

1. Preheat the air fryer to 400°F.

2. Set up and fill two shallow soup plates or small pie plates on your counter: one with the flour, whisked with the Old Bay until well combined; and one with the egg(s), whisked with the beer until foamy and uniform.

3. Dip a piece of cod in the flour mixture, turning it to coat on all sides (not just the top and bottom). Gently shake off any excess flour and dip the fish in the egg mixture, turning it to coat. Let any excess egg mixture slip back into the rest, then set the fish back in the flour mixture and coat it again, then back in the egg mixture for a second wash, then back in the flour mixture for a third time. Coat the fish on all sides with vegetable oil spray and set it aside. "Batter" the remaining piece(s) of cod in the same way.

4. Set the coated cod fillets in the basket with as much space between them as possible. They should not touch. Air-fry undisturbed for 12 minutes, or until brown and crisp.

5. Use kitchen tongs to gently transfer the fish to a wire rack. Cool for only a couple of minutes before serving.

Lime Halibut Parcels

Servings: 4

Cooking Time: 45 Minutes

Ingredients:

- 1 lime, sliced
- 4 halibut fillets
- 1 tsp dried thyme
- Salt and pepper to taste
- 1 shredded carrot
- 1 red bell pepper, sliced
- ½ cup sliced celery
- 2 tbsp butter

Directions:

1. Preheat the air fryer to 400°F. Tear off four 14-inch lengths of parchment paper and fold each piece in half crosswise. Put the lime slices in the center of half of each piece of paper, then top with halibut. Sprinkle each filet with thyme, salt, and pepper, then top each with ¼ of the carrots, bell pepper, and celery. Add a dab of butter. Fold the parchment paper in half and crimp the edges all around to enclose the halibut and vegetables. Put one parchment bundle in the basket, add a raised rack, and add another bundle. Bake for 12-14 minutes or until the bundle puff up. The fish should flake with a fork; put the bundles in the oven to keep warm. Repeat for the second batch of parchment bundles. Hot steam will be released when the bundles are opened.

Butternut Squash–wrapped Halibut Fillets

Servings:3

Cooking Time: 11 Minutes

Ingredients:

- 15 Long spiralized peeled and seeded butternut squash strands
- 3 5- to 6-ounce skinless halibut fillets
- 3 tablespoons Butter, melted
- ¾ teaspoon Mild paprika
- ¾ teaspoon Table salt
- ¾ teaspoon Ground black pepper

Directions:

1. Preheat the air fryer to 375°F .
2. Hold 5 long butternut squash strands together and wrap them around a fillet. Set it aside and wrap any remaining fillet(s).
3. Mix the melted butter, paprika, salt, and pepper in a small bowl. Brush this mixture over the squash-wrapped fillets on all sides.
4. When the machine is at temperature, set the fillets in the basket with as much air space between them as possible. Air-fry undisturbed for 10 minutes, or until the squash strands have browned but not burned. If the machine is at 360°F, you may need to add 1 minute to the cooking time. In any event, watch the fish carefully after the 8-minute mark.
5. Use a nonstick-safe spatula to gently transfer the fillets to a serving platter or plates. Cool for only a minute or so before serving.

Bacon-wrapped Scallops

Servings: 4

Cooking Time: 8 Minutes

Ingredients:

- 16 large scallops
- 8 bacon strips
- ½ teaspoon black pepper
- ¼ teaspoon smoked paprika

Directions:

1. Pat the scallops dry with a paper towel. Slice each of the bacon strips in half. Wrap 1 bacon strip around 1 scallop and secure with a toothpick. Repeat with the remaining scallops. Season the scallops with pepper and paprika.
2. Preheat the air fryer to 350°F.
3. Place the bacon-wrapped scallops in the air fryer basket and cook for 4 minutes, shake the basket, cook another 3 minutes, shake the basket, and cook another 1 to 3 to minutes. When the bacon is crispy, the scallops should be cooked through and slightly firm, but not rubbery. Serve immediately.

Lemon-dill Salmon With Green Beans

Servings: 4

Cooking Time: 20 Minutes

Ingredients:

- 20 halved cherry tomatoes
- 4 tbsp butter
- 4 garlic cloves, minced
- ¼ cup chopped dill
- Salt and pepper to taste
- 4 wild-caught salmon fillets
- ¼ cup white wine
- 1 lemon, thinly sliced
- 1 lb green beans, trimmed
- 2 tbsp chopped parsley

Directions:

1. Preheat air fryer to 390°F. Combine butter, garlic, dill, wine, salt, and pepper in a small bowl. Spread the seasoned butter over the top of the salmon. Arrange the fish in a single layer in the frying basket. Top with ½ of the lemon slices and surround the fish with green beans and tomatoes. Bake for 12-15 minutes until salmon is cooked and vegetables are tender. Top with parsley and serve with lemon slices on the side.

Easy Asian-style Tuna

Servings: 4

Cooking Time: 25 Minutes

Ingredients:

- 1 jalapeño pepper, minced
- ½ tsp Chinese five-spice
- 4 tuna steaks
- ½ tsp toasted sesame oil
- 2 garlic cloves, grated
- 1 tbsp grated fresh ginger
- Black pepper to taste
- 2 tbsp lemon juice

Directions:

1. Preheat air fryer to 380°F. Pour sesame oil over the tuna steaks and let them sit while you make the marinade. Combine the jalapeño, garlic, ginger, five-spice powder, black pepper, and lemon juice in a bowl, then brush the mix on the fish. Let it sit for 10 minutes. Air Fry the tuna in the fryer for 6-11 minutes until it is cooked through and flakes easily when pressed with a fork. Serve warm.

Oyster Shrimp With Fried Rice

Servings: 4

Cooking Time: 40 Minutes

Ingredients:

- 1 lb peeled shrimp, deveined
- 1 shallot, chopped
- 2 garlic cloves, minced
- 1 tbsp olive oil
- 1 tbsp butter
- 2 eggs, beaten
- 2 cups cooked rice
- 1 cup baby peas
- 2 tbsp fish sauce
- 1 tbsp oyster sauce

Directions:

1. Preheat the air fryer to 370°F. Combine the shrimp, shallot, garlic, and olive oil in a cake pan. Put the cake pan in the air fryer and Bake the shrimp for 5-7 minutes, stirring once until shrimp are no pinker. Remove into a bowl, and set aside. Put the butter in the hot cake pan to melt. Add the eggs and return to the fryer. Bake for 4-6 minutes, stirring once until the eggs are set. Remove the eggs from the pan and set aside.

2. Add the rice, peas, oyster sauce, and fish sauce to the pan and return it to the fryer. Bake for 12-15 minutes, stirring once halfway through. Pour in the shrimp and eggs and stir. Cook for 2-3 more minutes until everything is hot.

Tex-mex Fish Tacos

Servings:3

Cooking Time: 7 Minutes

Ingredients:

- ¾ teaspoon Chile powder
- ¼ teaspoon Ground cumin
- ¼ teaspoon Dried oregano
- 3 5-ounce skinless mahi-mahi fillets
- Vegetable oil spray
- 3 Corn or flour tortillas
- 6 tablespoons Diced tomatoes
- 3 tablespoons Regular, low-fat, or fat-free sour cream

Directions:

1. Preheat the air fryer to 400°F.

2. Stir the chile powder, cumin, and oregano in a small bowl until well combined.

3. Coat each piece of fish all over (even the sides and ends) with vegetable oil spray. Sprinkle the spice mixture evenly over all sides of the fillets. Lightly spray them again.

4. When the machine is at temperature, set the fillets in the basket with as much air space between them as possible. Air-fry undisturbed for 7 minutes, until lightly browned and firm but not hard.

5. Use a nonstick-safe spatula to transfer the fillets to a wire rack. Microwave the tortillas on high for a few seconds, until supple. Put a fillet in each tortilla and top each with 2 tablespoons diced tomatoes and 1 tablespoon sour cream.

Halibut Quesadillas

Servings: 2
Cooking Time: 30 Minutes
Ingredients:

- ¼ cup shredded cheddar
- ¼ cup shredded mozzarella
- 1 tsp olive oil
- 2 tortilla shells
- 1 halibut fillet
- ½ peeled avocado, sliced
- 1 garlic clove, minced
- Salt and pepper to taste
- ½ tsp lemon juice

Directions:

1. Preheat air fryer to 350°F. Brush the halibut fillet with olive oil and sprinkle with salt and pepper. Bake in the air fryer for 12-14 minutes, flipping once until cooked through. Combine the avocado, garlic, salt, pepper, and lemon juice in a bowl and, using a fork, mash lightly until the avocado is slightly chunky. Add and spread the resulting guacamole on one tortilla. Top with the cooked fish and cheeses, and cover with the second tortilla. Bake in the air fryer 6-8, flipping once until the cheese is melted. Serve immediately.

Cheese & Crab Stuffed Mushrooms

Servings: 2
Cooking Time: 30 Minutes
Ingredients:

- 6 oz lump crabmeat, shells discarded
- 6 oz mascarpone cheese, softened
- 2 jalapeño peppers, minced
- ¼ cup diced red onions
- 2 tsp grated Parmesan cheese
- 2 portobello mushroom caps
- 2 tbsp butter, divided
- ½ tsp prepared horseradish
- ¼ tsp Worcestershire sauce
- ¼ tsp smoked paprika
- Salt and pepper to taste
- ¼ cup bread crumbs

Directions:

1. Melt 1 tbsp of butter in a skillet over heat for 30 seconds. Add in onion and cook for 3 minutes until tender. Stir in mascarpone cheese, Parmesan cheese, horseradish, jalapeño peppers, Worcestershire sauce, paprika, salt and pepper and cook for 2 minutes until smooth. Fold in crabmeat. Spoon mixture into mushroom caps. Set aside.
2. Preheat air fryer at 350°F. Microwave the remaining butter until melted. Stir in breadcrumbs. Scatter over stuffed mushrooms. Place mushrooms in the greased frying basket and Bake for 8 minutes. Serve immediately.

Shrimp Al Pesto

Servings: 4

Cooking Time: 10 Minutes

Ingredients:

- 1 lb peeled shrimp, deveined
- ¼ cup pesto sauce
- 1 lime, sliced
- 2 cups cooked farro

Directions:

1. Preheat air fryer to 360°F. Coat the shrimp with the pesto sauce in a bowl. Put the shrimp in a single layer in the frying basket. Put the lime slices over the shrimp and Roast for 5 minutes. Remove lime and discard. Serve the shrimp over a bed of farro pilaf. Enjoy!

Fish Sticks With Tartar Sauce

Servings: 2

Cooking Time: 6 Minutes

Ingredients:

- 12 ounces cod or flounder
- ½ cup flour
- ½ teaspoon paprika
- 1 teaspoon salt
- lots of freshly ground black pepper
- 2 eggs, lightly beaten
- 1½ cups panko breadcrumbs
- 1 teaspoon salt
- vegetable oil
- Tartar Sauce:
- ¼ cup mayonnaise
- 2 teaspoons lemon juice
- 2 tablespoons finely chopped sweet pickles
- salt and freshly ground black pepper

Directions:

1. Cut the fish into ¾-inch wide sticks or strips. Set up a dredging station. Combine the flour, paprika, salt and pepper in a shallow dish. Beat the eggs lightly in a second shallow dish. Finally, mix the breadcrumbs and salt in a third shallow dish. Coat the fish sticks by dipping the fish into the flour, then the egg and finally the breadcrumbs, coating on all sides in each step and pressing the crumbs firmly onto the fish. Place the finished sticks on a plate or baking sheet while you finish all the sticks.
2. Preheat the air fryer to 400°F.
3. Spray the fish sticks with the oil and spray or brush the bottom of the air fryer basket. Place the fish into the basket and air-fry at 400°F for 4 minutes, turn the fish sticks over, and air-fry for another 2 minutes.
4. While the fish is cooking, mix the tartar sauce ingredients together.
5. Serve the fish sticks warm with the tartar sauce and some French fries on the side.

Honey Pecan Shrimp

Servings: 4

Cooking Time: 10 Minutes

Ingredients:

- ¼ cup cornstarch
- ¾ teaspoon sea salt, divided
- ¼ teaspoon pepper
- 2 egg whites
- ⅔ cup finely chopped pecans
- 1 pound raw, peeled, and deveined shrimp
- ¼ cup honey
- 2 tablespoons mayonnaise

Directions:

1. In a small bowl, whisk together the cornstarch, ½ teaspoon of the salt, and the pepper.

2. In a second bowl, whisk together the egg whites until soft and foamy. (They don't need to be whipped to peaks or even soft peaks, just frothy.)

3. In a third bowl, mix together the pecans and the remaining ¼ teaspoon of sea salt.

4. Pat the shrimp dry with paper towels. Working in small batches, dip the shrimp into the cornstarch, then into the egg whites, and then into the pecans until all the shrimp are coated with pecans.

5. Preheat the air fryer to 330°F.

6. Place the coated shrimp inside the air fryer basket and spray with cooking spray. Cook for 5 minutes, toss the shrimp, and cook another 5 minutes.

7. Meanwhile, place the honey in a microwave-safe bowl and microwave for 30 seconds. Whisk in the mayonnaise until smooth and creamy. Pour the honey sauce into a serving bowl. Add the cooked shrimp to the serving bowl while hot and toss to coat. Serve immediately.

Curried Sweet-and-spicy Scallops

Servings:3

Cooking Time: 5 Minutes

Ingredients:

- 6 tablespoons Thai sweet chili sauce
- 2 cups (from about 5 cups cereal) Crushed Rice Krispies or other rice-puff cereal
- 2 teaspoons Yellow curry powder, purchased or homemade (see here)
- 1 pound Sea scallops
- Vegetable oil spray

Directions:

1. Preheat the air fryer to 400°F.

2. Set up and fill two shallow soup plates or small pie plates on your counter: one for the chili sauce and one for crumbs, mixed with the curry powder.

3. Dip a scallop into the chili sauce, coating it on all sides. Set it in the cereal mixture and turn several times to coat evenly. Gently shake off any excess and set the scallop on a cutting board. Continue dipping and coating the remaining scallops. Coat them all on all sides with the vegetable oil spray.

4. Set the scallops in the basket with as much air space between them as possible. Air-fry undisturbed for 5 minutes, or until lightly browned and crunchy.

5. Remove the basket. Set aside for 2 minutes to let the coating set up. Then gently pour the contents of the basket onto a platter and serve at once.

Chapter 5 Vegetarians Recipes

Egg Rolls

Servings: 4
Cooking Time: 8 Minutes
Ingredients:

- 1 clove garlic, minced
- 1 teaspoon sesame oil
- 1 teaspoon olive oil
- ½ cup chopped celery
- ½ cup grated carrots
- 2 green onions, chopped
- 2 ounces mushrooms, chopped
- 2 cups shredded Napa cabbage
- 1 teaspoon low-sodium soy sauce
- 1 teaspoon cornstarch
- salt
- 1 egg
- 1 tablespoon water
- 4 egg roll wraps
- olive oil for misting or cooking spray

Directions:

1. In a large skillet, sauté garlic in sesame and olive oils over medium heat for 1 minute.
2. Add celery, carrots, onions, and mushrooms to skillet. Cook 1 minute, stirring.
3. Stir in cabbage, cover, and cook for 1 minute or just until cabbage slightly wilts.
4. In a small bowl, mix soy sauce and cornstarch. Stir into vegetables to thicken. Remove from heat. Salt to taste if needed.
5. Beat together egg and water in a small bowl.
6. Divide filling into 4 portions and roll up in egg roll wraps. Brush all over with egg wash to seal.
7. Mist egg rolls very lightly with olive oil or cooking spray and place in air fryer basket.
8. Cook at 390°F for 4minutes. Turn over and cook 4 more minutes, until golden brown and crispy.

Crispy Apple Fries With Caramel Sauce

Servings: 4
Cooking Time: 15 Minutes
Ingredients:

- 4 medium apples, cored
- ¼ tsp cinnamon
- ¼ tsp nutmeg
- 1 cup caramel sauce

Directions:

1. Preheat air fryer to 350°F. Slice the apples to a 1/3-inch thickness for a crunchy chip. Place in a large bowl and sprinkle with cinnamon and nutmeg. Place the slices in the air fryer basket. Bake for 6 minutes. Shake the basket, then cook for another 4 minutes or until crunchy. Serve drizzled with caramel sauce and enjoy!

Mushroom Bolognese Casserole

Servings: 4

Cooking Time: 20 Minutes

Ingredients:

- 1 cup canned diced tomatoes
- 2 garlic cloves, minced
- 1 tsp onion powder
- ¾ tsp dried basil
- ¾ tsp dried oregano
- 1 cup chopped mushrooms
- 16 oz cooked spaghetti

Directions:

1. Preheat air fryer to 400°F. Whisk the tomatoes and their juices, garlic, onion powder, basil, oregano, and mushrooms in a baking pan. Cover with aluminum foil and Bake for 6 minutes. Slide out the pan and add the cooked spaghetti; stir to coat. Cover with aluminum foil and Bake for 3 minutes until and bubbly. Serve and enjoy!

Chili Tofu & Quinoa Bowls

Servings: 2

Cooking Time: 30 Minutes

Ingredients:

- 1 cup diced peeled sweet potatoes
- ¼ cup chopped mixed bell peppers
- 1/8 cup sprouted green lentils
- ½ onion, sliced
- 1 tsp avocado oil
- 1/8 cup chopped carrots
- 8 oz extra-firm tofu, cubed
- ½ tsp smoked paprika
- ½ tsp chili powder
- ¼ tsp salt
- 2 tsp lime zest
- 1 cup cooked quinoa
- 2 lime wedges

Directions:

1. Preheat air fryer at 350ºF. Combine the onion, carrots, bell peppers, green lentils, sweet potato, and avocado oil in a bowl. In another bowl, mix the tofu, paprika, chili powder, and salt. Add veggie mixture to the frying basket and Air Fry for 8 minutes. Stir in tofu mixture and cook for 8 more minutes. Combine lime zest and quinoa. Divide into 2 serving bowls. Top each with the tofu mixture and squeeze a lime wedge over. Serve warm.

Tropical Salsa

Servings: 4
Cooking Time: 15 Minutes
Ingredients:

- 1 cup pineapple cubes
- ½ apple, cubed
- Salt to taste
- ¼ tsp olive oil
- 2 tomatoes, diced
- 1 avocado, diced
- 3-4 strawberries, diced
- ¼ cup diced red onion
- 1 tbsp chopped cilantro
- 1 tbsp chopped parsley
- 2 cloves garlic, minced
- ½ tsp granulated sugar
- ½ lime, juiced

Directions:

1. Preheat air fryer at 400ºF. Combine pineapple cubes, apples, olive oil, and salt in a bowl. Place pineapple in the greased frying basket, and Air Fry for 8 minutes, shaking once. Transfer it to a bowl. Toss in tomatoes, avocado, strawberries, onion, cilantro, parsley, garlic, sugar, lime juice, and salt. Let chill in the fridge before using.

Sweet Corn Bread

Servings: 6
Cooking Time: 35 Minutes
Ingredients:

- 2 eggs, beaten
- ½ cup cornmeal
- ½ cup pastry flour
- 1/3 cup sugar
- 1 tsp lemon zest
- ½ tbsp baking powder
- ¼ tsp salt
- ¼ tsp baking soda
- ½ tbsp lemon juice
- ½ cup milk
- ¼ cup sunflower oil

Directions:

1. Preheat air fryer to 350°F. Add the cornmeal, flour, sugar, lemon zest, baking powder, salt, and baking soda in a bowl. Stir with a whisk until combined. Add the eggs, lemon juice, milk, and oil to another bowl and stir well. Add the wet mixture to the dry mixture and stir gently until combined. Spray a baking pan with oil. Pour the batter in and Bake in the fryer for 25 minutes or until golden and a knife inserted in the center comes out clean. Cut into wedges and serve.

Thai Peanut Veggie Burgers

Servings: 6

Cooking Time: 14 Minutes

Ingredients:

- One 15.5-ounce can cannellini beans
- 1 teaspoon minced garlic
- ¼ cup chopped onion
- 1 Thai chili pepper, sliced
- 2 tablespoons natural peanut butter
- ½ teaspoon black pepper
- ½ teaspoon salt
- ⅓ cup all-purpose flour (optional)
- ½ cup cooked quinoa
- 1 large carrot, grated
- 1 cup shredded red cabbage
- ¼ cup peanut dressing
- ¼ cup chopped cilantro
- 6 Hawaiian rolls
- 6 butterleaf lettuce leaves

Directions:

1. Preheat the air fryer to 350°F.

2. To a blender or food processor fitted with a metal blade, add the beans, garlic, onion, chili pepper, peanut butter, pepper, and salt. Pulse for 5 to 10 seconds. Do not over process. The mixture should be coarse, not smooth.

3. Remove from the blender or food processor and spoon into a large bowl. Mix in the cooked quinoa and carrots. At this point, the mixture should begin to hold together to form small patties. If the dough appears to be too sticky (meaning you likely processed a little too long), add the flour to hold the patties together.

4. Using a large spoon, form 8 equal patties out of the batter.

5. Liberally spray a metal trivet with olive oil spray and set in the air fryer basket. Place the patties into the basket, leaving enough space to be able to turn them with a spatula.

6. Cook for 7 minutes, flip, and cook another 7 minutes.

7. Remove from the heat and repeat with additional patties.

8. To serve, place the red cabbage in a bowl and toss with peanut dressing and cilantro. Place the veggie burger on a bun, and top with a slice of lettuce and cabbage slaw.

Spaghetti Squash And Kale Fritters With Pomodoro Sauce

Servings: 3

Cooking Time: 45 Minutes

Ingredients:

- 1½-pound spaghetti squash (about half a large or a whole small squash)
- olive oil
- ½ onion, diced
- ½ red bell pepper, diced
- 2 cloves garlic, minced
- 4 cups coarsely chopped kale
- salt and freshly ground black pepper
- 1 egg
- ⅓ cup breadcrumbs, divided*
- ⅓ cup grated Parmesan cheese
- ½ teaspoon dried rubbed sage
- pinch nutmeg
- Pomodoro Sauce:
- 2 tablespoons olive oil
- ½ onion, chopped
- 1 to 2 cloves garlic, minced
- 1 (28-ounce) can peeled tomatoes
- ¼ cup red wine
- 1 teaspoon Italian seasoning
- 2 tablespoons chopped fresh basil, plus more for garnish
- salt and freshly ground black pepper
- ½ teaspoon sugar (optional)

Directions:

1. Preheat the air fryer to 370°F.

2. Cut the spaghetti squash in half lengthwise and remove the seeds. Rub the inside of the squash with olive oil and season with salt and pepper. Place the squash, cut side up, into the air fryer basket and air-fry for 30 minutes, flipping the squash over halfway through the cooking process.

3. While the squash is cooking, Preheat a large sauté pan over medium heat on the stovetop. Add a little olive oil and sauté the onions for 3 minutes, until they start to soften. Add the red pepper and garlic and continue to sauté for an additional 4 minutes. Add the kale and season with salt and pepper. Cook for 2 more minutes, or until the kale is soft. Transfer the mixture to a large bowl and let it cool.

4. While the squash continues to cook, make the Pomodoro sauce. Preheat the large sauté pan again over medium heat on the stovetop. Add the olive oil and sauté the onion and garlic for 2 to 3 minutes, until the onion begins to soften. Crush the canned tomatoes with your hands and add them to the pan along with the red wine and Italian seasoning and simmer for 20 minutes. Add the basil and season to taste with salt, pepper and sugar (if using).

5. When the spaghetti squash has finished cooking, use a fork to scrape the inside flesh of the squash onto a sheet pan. Spread the squash out and let it cool.

6. Once cool, add the spaghetti squash to the kale mixture, along with the egg, breadcrumbs, Parmesan cheese, sage, nutmeg, salt and freshly ground black pepper. Stir to combine well and then divide the mixture into 6 thick portions. You can shape the portions into patties, but I prefer to keep them a little random and unique in shape. Spray or brush the fritters with olive oil.

7. Preheat the air fryer to 370°F.

8. Brush the air fryer basket with a little olive oil and transfer the fritters to the basket. Air-fry the squash and kale fritters at 370°F for 15 minutes, flipping them over halfway through the cooking process.

9. Serve the fritters warm with the Pomodoro sauce spooned over the top or pooled on your plate. Garnish with the fresh basil leaves.

Vegetable Couscous

Servings: 4

Cooking Time: 10 Minutes

Ingredients:

- 4 ounces white mushrooms, sliced
- ½ medium green bell pepper, julienned
- 1 cup cubed zucchini
- ¼ small onion, slivered
- 1 stalk celery, thinly sliced
- ¼ teaspoon ground coriander
- ¼ teaspoon ground cumin
- salt and pepper
- 1 tablespoon olive oil
- Couscous
- ¾ cup uncooked couscous
- 1 cup vegetable broth or water
- ½ teaspoon salt (omit if using salted broth)

Directions:

1. Combine all vegetables in large bowl. Sprinkle with coriander, cumin, and salt and pepper to taste. Stir well, add olive oil, and stir again to coat vegetables evenly.

2. Place vegetables in air fryer basket and cook at 390°F for 5minutes. Stir and cook for 5 more minutes, until tender.

3. While vegetables are cooking, prepare the couscous: Place broth or water and salt in large saucepan. Heat to boiling, stir in couscous, cover, and remove from heat.

4. Let couscous sit for 5minutes, stir in cooked vegetables, and serve hot.

Garlic Okra Chips

Servings: 4

Cooking Time: 20 Minutes

Ingredients:

- 2 cups okra, cut into rounds
- 1 ½ tbsp. melted butter
- 1 garlic clove, minced
- 1 tsp powdered paprika
- Salt and pepper to taste

Directions:

1. Preheat air fryer to 350°F. Toss okra, melted butter, paprika, garlic, salt and pepper in a medium bowl until okra is coated. Place okra in the frying basket and Air Fry for 5 minutes. Shake the basket and Air Fry for another 5 minutes. Shake one more time and Air Fry for 2 minutes until crispy. Serve warm and enjoy.

Veggie-stuffed Bell Peppers

Servings:4
Cooking Time: 40 Minutes
Ingredients:

- ½ cup canned fire-roasted diced tomatoes, including juice
- 2 red bell peppers
- 4 tsp olive oil
- ½ yellow onion, diced
- 1 zucchini, diced
- ¾ cup chopped mushrooms
- ¼ cup tomato sauce
- 2 tsp Italian seasoning
- ¼ tsp smoked paprika
- Salt and pepper to taste

Directions:

1. Cut bell peppers in half from top to bottom and discard the seeds. Brush inside and tops of the bell peppers with some olive oil. Set aside. Warm the remaining olive oil in a skillet over medium heat. Stir-fry the onion, zucchini, and mushrooms for 5 minutes until the onions are tender. Combine tomatoes and their juice, tomato sauce, Italian seasoning, paprika, salt, and pepper in a bowl.

2. Preheat air fryer to 350ºF. Divide both mixtures between bell pepper halves. Place bell pepper halves in the frying basket and Air Fry for 8 minutes. Serve immediately.

Veggie Samosas

Servings: 6
Cooking Time: 30 Minutes
Ingredients:

- 2 tbsp cream cheese, softened
- 3 tbsp minced onion
- 2 garlic cloves, minced
- 2 tbsp grated carrots
- 3 tsp olive oil
- 3 tbsp cooked green lentils
- 6 phyllo dough sheets

Directions:

1. Preheat air fryer to 390°F. Toss the onion, garlic, carrots, and some oil in a baking pan and stir. Place in the fryer and Air Fry for 2-4 minutes until the veggies are soft. Pour into a bowl. Add the lentils and cream cheese; let chill.

2. To make the dough, first lay a sheet of phyllo on a clean workspace and spritz with some olive oil, then add a second sheet on top. Repeat with the rest of the phyllo sheets until you have 3 stacks of 2 layers. Cut the stacks into 4 lengthwise strips. Add 2 tsp of the veggie mix at the bottom of each strip, then make a triangle by lifting one corner over the filling. Continue the triangle making, like folding a flag, and seal with water. Repeat until all strips are filled and folded. Bake the samosas in the air fryer for 4-7 minutes, until golden and crisp. Serve warm.

Zucchini & Bell Pepper Stir-fry

Servings: 4

Cooking Time: 25 Minutes

Ingredients:

- 1 zucchini, cut into rounds
- 1 red bell pepper, sliced
- 3 garlic cloves, sliced
- 2 tbsp olive oil
- 1/3 cup vegetable broth
- 1 tbsp lemon juice
- 2 tsp cornstarch
- 1 tsp dried basil
- Salt and pepper to taste

Directions:

1. Preheat the air fryer to 400°F. Combine the veggies, garlic, and olive oil in a bowl. Put the bowl in the frying basket and Air Fry the zucchini mixture for 5 minutes, stirring once; drain. While the veggies are cooking, whisk the broth, lemon juice, cornstarch, basil, salt, and pepper in a bowl. Pour the broth into the bowl along with the veggies and stir. Air Fry for 5-9 more minutes until the veggies are tender and the sauce is thick. Serve and enjoy!

Vegetarian Eggplant "pizzas"

Servings:4

Cooking Time: 25 Minutes

Ingredients:

- ½ cup diced baby bella mushrooms
- 3 tbsp olive oil
- ¼ cup diced onions
- ½ cup pizza sauce
- 1 eggplant, sliced
- 1 tsp salt
- 1 cup shredded mozzarella
- ¼ cup chopped oregano

Directions:

1. Warm 2 tsp of olive oil in a skillet over medium heat. Add in onion and mushrooms and stir-fry for 4 minutes until tender. Stir in pizza sauce. Turn the heat off.

2. Preheat air fryer to 375°F. Brush the eggplant slices with the remaining olive oil on both sides. Lay out slices on a large plate and season with salt. Then, top with the sauce mixture and shredded mozzarella. Place the eggplant pizzas in the frying basket and Air Fry for 5 minutes. Garnish with oregano to serve.

Quinoa Green Pizza

Servings: 2

Cooking Time: 25 Minutes

Ingredients:

- ¾ cup quinoa flour
- ½ tsp dried basil
- ½ tsp dried oregano
- 1 tbsp apple cider vinegar
- 1/3 cup ricotta cheese
- 2/3 cup chopped broccoli
- ½ tsp garlic powder

Directions:

1. Preheat air fryer to 350°F. Whisk quinoa flour, basil, oregano, apple cider vinegar, and ½ cup of water until smooth. Set aside. Cut 2 pieces of parchment paper. Place the quinoa mixture on one paper, top with another piece, and flatten to create a crust. Discard the top piece of paper. Bake for 5 minutes, turn and discard the other piece of paper. Spread the ricotta cheese over the crust, scatter with broccoli, and sprinkle with garlic. Grill at 400°F for 5 minutes until golden brown. Serve warm.

Basil Green Beans

Servings: 4

Cooking Time: 15 Minutes

Ingredients:

- 1 ½ lb green beans, trimmed
- 1 tbsp olive oil
- 1 tbsp fresh basil, chopped
- Garlic salt to taste

Directions:

1. Preheat air fryer to 400°F. Coat the green beans with olive oil in a large bowl. Combine with fresh basil powder and garlic salt. Put the beans in the frying basket and Air Fry for 7-9 minutes, shaking once until the beans begin to brown. Serve warm and enjoy!

Colorful Vegetable Medley

Servings: 4

Cooking Time: 20 Minutes

Ingredients:

- 1 lb green beans, chopped
- 2 carrots, cubed
- Salt and pepper to taste
- 1 zucchini, cut into chunks
- 1 red bell pepper, sliced

Directions:

1. Preheat air fryer to 390°F. Combine green beans, carrots, salt and pepper in a large bowl. Spray with cooking oil and transfer to the frying basket. Roast for 6 minutes.

2. Combine zucchini and red pepper in a bowl. Season to taste and spray with cooking oil; set aside. When the cooking time is up, add the zucchini and red pepper to the basket. Cook for another 6 minutes. Serve and enjoy.

Veggie Burgers

Servings: 4

Cooking Time: 15 Minutes

Ingredients:

- 2 cans black beans, rinsed and drained
- ½ cup cooked quinoa
- ½ cup shredded raw sweet potato
- ¼ cup diced red onion
- 2 teaspoons ground cumin
- 1 teaspoon coriander powder
- ½ teaspoon salt
- oil for misting or cooking spray
- 8 slices bread
- suggested toppings: lettuce, tomato, red onion, Pepper Jack cheese, guacamole

Directions:

1. In a medium bowl, mash the beans with a fork.
2. Add the quinoa, sweet potato, onion, cumin, coriander, and salt and mix well with the fork.
3. Shape into 4 patties, each ¾-inch thick.
4. Mist both sides with oil or cooking spray and also mist the basket.
5. Cook at 390°F for 15minutes.
6. Follow the recipe for Toast, Plain & Simple.
7. Pop the veggie burgers back in the air fryer for a minute or two to reheat if necessary.
8. Serve on the toast with your favorite burger toppings.

Two-cheese Grilled Sandwiches

Servings: 2

Cooking Time: 30 Minutes

Ingredients:

- 4 sourdough bread slices
- 2 cheddar cheese slices
- 2 Swiss cheese slices
- 1 tbsp butter
- 2 dill pickles, sliced

Directions:

1. Preheat air fryer to 360°F. Smear both sides of the sourdough bread with butter and place them in the frying basket. Toast the bread for 6 minutes, flipping once.

2. Divide the cheddar cheese between 2 of the bread slices. Cover the remaining 2 bread slices with Swiss cheese slices. Bake for 10 more minutes until the cheeses have melted and lightly bubbled and the bread has golden brown. Set the cheddar-covered bread slices on a serving plate, cover with pickles, and top each with the Swiss-covered slices. Serve and enjoy!

Authentic Mexican Esquites

Servings: 4
Cooking Time: 25 Minutes
Ingredients:

- 4 ears of corn, husk and silk removed
- 1 tbsp ground coriander
- 1 tbsp smoked paprika
- 1 tsp sea salt
- 1 tsp garlic powder
- 1 tsp onion powder
- 1 tsp dried lime peel
- 1 tsp cayenne pepper
- 3 tbsp mayonnaise
- 3 tbsp grated Cotija cheese
- 1 tbsp butter, melted
- 1 tsp epazote seasoning

Directions:

1. Preheat the air fryer to 400°F. Combine the coriander, paprika, salt, garlic powder, onion powder, lime peel, epazote and cayenne pepper in a small bowl and mix well. Pour into a small glass jar. Put the corn in the greased frying basket and Bake for 6-8 minutes or until the corn is crispy but tender. Make sure to rearrange the ears halfway through cooking.
2. While the corn is frying, combine the mayonnaise, cheese, and melted butter in a small bowl. Spread the mixture over the cooked corn, return to the fryer, and Bake for 3-5 minutes more or until the corn has brown spots. Remove from the fryer and sprinkle each cob with about ½ tsp of the spice mix.

Chapter 6 Vegetable Side Dishes Recipes

Chili-oiled Brussels Sprouts

Servings: 4
Cooking Time: 30 Minutes
Ingredients:

- 1 cup Brussels sprouts, quartered
- 1 tsp olive oil
- 1 tsp chili oil
- Salt and pepper to taste

Directions:

1. Preheat air fryer to 350°F. Coat the Brussels sprouts with olive oil, chili oil, salt, and black pepper in a bowl. Transfer to the frying basket. Bake for 20 minutes, shaking the basket several times throughout cooking until the sprouts are crispy, browned on the outside, and juicy inside. Serve and enjoy!

Stuffed Avocados

Servings: 4

Cooking Time: 8 Minutes

Ingredients:

- 1 cup frozen shoepeg corn, thawed
- 1 cup cooked black beans
- ¼ cup diced onion
- ½ teaspoon cumin
- 2 teaspoons lime juice, plus extra for serving
- salt and pepper
- 2 large avocados, split in half, pit removed

Directions:

1. Mix together the corn, beans, onion, cumin, and lime juice. Season to taste with salt and pepper.
2. Scoop out some of the flesh from center of each avocado and set aside. Divide corn mixture evenly between the cavities.
3. Set avocado halves in air fryer basket and cook at 360°F for 8 minutes, until corn mixture is hot.
4. Season the avocado flesh that you scooped out with a squirt of lime juice, salt, and pepper. Spoon it over the cooked halves.

Layered Mixed Vegetables

Servings: 4

Cooking Time: 30 Minutes

Ingredients:

- 1 Yukon Gold potato, sliced
- 1 eggplant, sliced
- 1 carrot, thinly sliced
- ¼ cup minced onions
- 3 garlic cloves, minced
- ¾ cup milk
- 2 tbsp cornstarch
- ½ tsp dried thyme

Directions:

1. Preheat air fryer to 380°F. In layers, add the potato, eggplant, carrot, onion, and garlic to a baking pan. Combine the milk, cornstarch, and thyme in a bowl, then pour this mix over the veggies. Put the pan in the air fryer and Bake for 15 minutes. The casserole should be golden on top with softened veggies. Serve immediately.

Vegetable Roast

Servings: 6

Cooking Time: 20 Minutes

Ingredients:

- 2 tbsp dill, chopped
- 2 zucchini, cubed
- 1 red bell pepper, diced
- 2 garlic cloves, sliced
- 2 tbsp olive oil
- ½ tsp salt
- ½ tsp red pepper flakes

Directions:

1.   Preheat air fryer to 380°F. Combine the zucchini, bell pepper, red pepper flakes, dill and garlic with olive oil and salt in a bowl. Pour the mixture into the frying basket and Roast for 14-16 minutes, shaking once. Serve warm.

Carrots & Parsnips With Tahini Sauce

Servings:4

Cooking Time: 20 Minutes

Ingredients:

- 2 parsnips, cut into half-moons
- 2 tsp olive oil
- ½ tsp salt
- 1 carrot, cut into sticks
- 1 tbsp tahini
- 1 tbsp lemon juice
- 1 clove garlic, minced
- 1 tbsp chopped parsley

Directions:

1.   Preheat air fryer to 375°F. Coat the parsnips and carrots with some olive oil and salt. Place them in the frying basket and Air Fry for 10 minutes, tossing once. In a bowl, whisk tahini, lemon juice, 1 tsp of water, and garlic. Pour the sauce over the cooked veggies. Scatter with parsley and serve.

Greek-inspired Ratatouille

Servings: 6

Cooking Time: 55 Minutes

Ingredients:

- 1 cup cherry tomatoes
- ½ bulb fennel, finely sliced
- 2 russet potatoes, cubed
- ½ cup tomatoes, cubed
- 1 eggplant, cubed
- 1 zucchini, cubed
- 1 red onion, chopped
- 1 red bell pepper, chopped
- 2 garlic cloves, minced
- 1 tsp dried mint
- 1 tsp dried parsley
- 1 tsp dried oregano
- Salt and pepper to taste
- ¼ tsp red pepper flakes
- 1/3 cup olive oil
- 1 can tomato paste
- ¼ cup vegetable broth

Directions:

1. Preheat air fryer to 320°F. Mix the potatoes, tomatoes, fennel, eggplant, zucchini, onion, bell pepper, garlic, mint, parsley, oregano, salt, black pepper, and red pepper flakes in a bowl. Whisk the olive oil, tomato paste, broth, and ¼ cup of water in a small bowl. Toss the mixture with the vegetables.

2. Pour the coated vegetables into the air frying basket in a single layer and Roast for 20 minutes. Stir well and spread out again. Roast for an additional 10 minutes, then repeat the process and cook for another 10 minutes. Serve and enjoy!

Sweet Potato Fries

Servings: 3

Cooking Time: 20 Minutes

Ingredients:

- 2 10-ounce sweet potato(es)
- Vegetable oil spray
- To taste Coarse sea salt or kosher salt

Directions:

1. Preheat the air fryer to 400°F.

2. Peel the sweet potato(es), then cut lengthwise into ¼-inch-thick slices. Cut these slices lengthwise into ¼-inch-thick matchsticks. Place these matchsticks in a bowl and coat them with vegetable oil spray. Toss well, spray them again, and toss several times to make sure they're all evenly coated.

3. When the machine is at temperature, pour the sweet potato matchsticks into the basket, spreading them out in as close to an even layer as possible. Air-fry for 20 minutes, tossing and rearranging the matchsticks every 5 minutes, until lightly browned and crisp.

4. Pour the contents of the basket into a bowl, add some salt to taste, and toss well to coat.

Roast Sweet Potatoes With Parmesan

Servings: 4

Cooking Time: 30 Minutes

Ingredients:

- 2 peeled sweet potatoes, sliced
- ¼ cup grated Parmesan
- 1 tsp olive oil
- 1 tbsp balsamic vinegar
- 1 tsp dried rosemary

Directions:

1. Preheat air fryer to 400°F. Place the sweet potatoes and some olive oil in a bowl and shake to coat. Spritz with balsamic vinegar and rosemary, then shake again. Put the potatoes in the frying basket and Roast for 18-25 minutes, shaking at least once until the potatoes are soft. Sprinkle with Parmesan cheese and serve warm.

Rosemary Roasted Potatoes With Lemon

Cooking Time: 12 Minutes

Servings: 4

Ingredients:

- 1 pound small red-skinned potatoes, halved or cut into bite-sized chunks
- 1 tablespoon olive oil
- 1 teaspoon finely chopped fresh rosemary
- ¼ teaspoon salt
- freshly ground black pepper
- 1 tablespoon lemon zest

Directions:

1. Preheat the air fryer to 400°F.
2. Toss the potatoes with the olive oil, rosemary, salt and freshly ground black pepper.
3. Air-fry for 12 minutes (depending on the size of the chunks), tossing the potatoes a few times throughout the cooking process.
4. As soon as the potatoes are tender to a knifepoint, toss them with the lemon zest and more salt if desired.

Buttery Stuffed Tomatoes

Servings: 6

Cooking Time: 15 Minutes

Ingredients:

- 3 8-ounce round tomatoes
- ½ cup plus 1 tablespoon Plain panko bread crumbs (gluten-free, if a concern)
- 3 tablespoons (about ½ ounce) Finely grated Parmesan cheese
- 3 tablespoons Butter, melted and cooled
- 4 teaspoons Stemmed and chopped fresh parsley leaves
- 1 teaspoon Minced garlic
- ¼ teaspoon Table salt
- Up to ¼ teaspoon Red pepper flakes
- Olive oil spray

Directions:

1. Preheat the air fryer to 375°F .

2. Cut the tomatoes in half through their "equators" (that is, not through the stem ends). One at a time, gently squeeze the tomato halves over a trash can, using a clean finger to gently force out the seeds and most of the juice inside, working carefully so that the tomato doesn't lose its round shape or get crushed.

3. Stir the bread crumbs, cheese, butter, parsley, garlic, salt, and red pepper flakes in a bowl until the bread crumbs are moistened and the parsley is uniform throughout the mixture. Pile this mixture into the spaces left in the tomato halves. Press gently to compact the filling. Coat the tops of the tomatoes with olive oil spray.

4. Place the tomatoes cut side up in the basket. They may touch each other. Air-fry for 15 minutes, or until the filling is lightly browned and crunchy.

5. Use nonstick-safe spatula and kitchen tongs for balance to gently transfer the stuffed tomatoes to a platter or a cutting board. Cool for a couple of minutes before serving.

Blistered Shishito Peppers

Servings:2

Cooking Time: 15 Minutes

Ingredients:

- 20 shishito peppers
- 1 tsp sesame oil
- ½ tsp soy sauce
- ½ tsp grated ginger
- Salt to taste
- 1 tsp sesame seeds

Directions:

1. Preheat air fryer to 375ºF. Coat the peppers with sesame oil and salt in a bowl. Transfer them to the frying basket and Air Fry for 8 minutes or until blistered and softened, shaking the basket to turn the peppers. Drizzle with soy sauce and sprinkle with ginger and sesame seeds to serve.

Summer Watermelon And Cucumber Salad

Servings: 4

Cooking Time: 15 Minutes

Ingredients:

- ½ red onion, sliced into half-moons
- 2 tbsp crumbled goat cheese
- 10 chopped basil leaves
- 4 cups watermelon cubes
- ½ cucumber, sliced
- 4 tsp olive oil
- Salt and pepper to taste
- 3 cups arugula
- 1 tsp balsamic vinegar
- 1 tsp honey
- 1 tbsp chopped mint

Directions:

1. Preheat air fryer at 375ºF. Toss watermelon, cucumber, onion, 2 tsp of olive oil, salt, and pepper in a bowl. Place it in the frying basket and Air Fry for 4 minutes, tossing once. In a salad bowl, whisk the arugula, balsamic vinegar, honey, and the remaining olive oil until the arugula is coated. Add in watermelon mixture. Scatter with goat cheese, basil leaves and mint to serve.

Balsamic Green Beans With Bacon

Servings:4

Cooking Time: 15 Minutes

Ingredients:

- 2 cups green beans, trimmed
- 1 tbsp butter, melted
- Salt and pepper to taste
- 1 bacon slice, diced
- 1 clove garlic, minced
- 1 tbsp balsamic vinegar

Directions:

1. Preheat air fryer to 375ºF. Combine green beans, butter, salt, and pepper in a bowl. Put the bean mixture in the frying basket and Air Fry for 5 minutes. Stir in bacon and Air Fry for 4 more minutes. Mix in garlic and cook for 1 minute. Transfer it to a serving dish, drizzle with balsamic vinegar and combine. Serve right away.

Mouth-watering Provençal Mushrooms

Servings: 4
Cooking Time: 35 Minutes
Ingredients:

- 2 lb mushrooms, quartered
- 2-3 tbsp olive oil
- ½ tsp garlic powder
- 2 tsp herbs de Provence
- 2 tbsp dry white wine

Directions:

1. Preheat air fryer to 320°F. Beat together the olive oil, garlic powder, herbs de Provence, and white wine in a bowl. Add the mushrooms and toss gently to coat. Spoon the mixture onto the frying basket and Bake for 16-18 minutes, stirring twice. Serve hot and enjoy!

Truffle Vegetable Croquettes

Servings: 4
Cooking Time: 40 Minutes
Ingredients:

- 2 cooked potatoes, mashed
- 1 cooked carrot, mashed
- 1 tbsp onion, minced
- 2 eggs, beaten
- 2 tbsp melted butter
- 1 tbsp truffle oil
- ½ tbsp flour
- Salt and pepper to taste

Directions:

1. Preheat air fryer to 350°F. Sift the flour, salt, and pepper in a bowl and stir to combine. Add the potatoes, carrot, onion, butter, and truffle oil to a separate bowl and mix well. Shape the potato mixture into small bite-sized patties. Dip the potato patties into the beaten eggs, coating thoroughly, then roll in the flour mixture to cover all sides. Arrange the croquettes in the greased frying basket and Air Fry for 14-16 minutes. Halfway through cooking, shake the basket. The croquettes should be crispy and golden. Serve hot and enjoy!

Roasted Broccoli And Red Bean Salad

Servings: 3

Cooking Time: 14 Minutes

Ingredients:

- 3 cups (about 1 pound) 1- to 1½-inch fresh broccoli florets (not frozen)
- 1½ tablespoons Olive oil spray
- 1¼ cups Canned red kidney beans, drained and rinsed
- 3 tablespoons Minced yellow or white onion
- 2 tablespoons plus 1 teaspoon Red wine vinegar
- ¾ teaspoon Dried oregano
- ¼ teaspoon Table salt
- ¼ teaspoon Ground black pepper

Directions:

1. Preheat the air fryer to 375°F .
2. Put the broccoli florets in a big bowl, coat them generously with olive oil spray, then toss to coat all surfaces, even down into the crannies, spraying them a couple of times more.
3. Pour the florets into the basket, spreading them into as close to one layer as you can. Air-fry for 12 minutes, tossing and rearranging the florets twice so that any touching or covered parts are eventually exposed to the air currents, until light browned but still a bit firm. (If the machine is at 360°F, you may need to add 2 minutes to the cooking time.)
4. Dump the contents of the basket onto a large cutting board. Cool for a minute or two, then chop the florets into small bits. Scrape these into a bowl and add the kidney beans, onion, vinegar, oregano, salt, and pepper. Toss well and serve warm or at room temperature.

Broccoli Tots

Servings: 24

Cooking Time: 10 Minutes

Ingredients:

- 2 cups broccoli florets (about ½ pound broccoli crowns)
- 1 egg, beaten
- ⅛ teaspoon onion powder
- ¼ teaspoon salt
- ⅛ teaspoon pepper
- 2 tablespoons grated Parmesan cheese
- ¼ cup panko breadcrumbs
- oil for misting

Directions:

1. Steam broccoli for 2minutes. Rinse in cold water, drain well, and chop finely.
2. In a large bowl, mix broccoli with all other ingredients except the oil.
3. Scoop out small portions of mixture and shape into 24 tots. Lay them on a cookie sheet or wax paper as you work.
4. Spray tots with oil and place in air fryer basket in single layer.
5. Cook at 390°F for 5minutes. Shake basket and spray with oil again. Cook 5minutes longer or until browned and crispy.

Spiced Roasted Acorn Squash

Servings: 2
Cooking Time: 45 Minutes
Ingredients:

- ½ acorn squash half
- 1 tsp butter, melted
- 2 tsp light brown sugar
- 1/8 tsp ground cinnamon
- 2 tbsp hot sauce
- ¼ cup maple syrup

Directions:

1. Preheat air fryer at 400ºF. Slice off about ¼-inch from the side of the squash half to sit flat like a bowl. In a bowl, combine all ingredients. Brush over the top of the squash and pour any remaining mixture in the middle of the squash. Place squash in the frying basket and Roast for 35 minutes. Cut it in half and divide between 2 serving plates. Serve.

Pecorino Dill Muffins

Servings:4
Cooking Time: 25 Minutes
Ingredients:

- ¼ cup grated Pecorino cheese
- 1 cup flour
- 1 tsp dried dill
- ⅛ tsp salt
- ¼ tsp onion powder
- 2 tsp baking powder
- 1 egg
- ¼ cup Greek yogurt

Directions:

1. Preheat air fryer to 350ºF. In a bowl, combine dry the ingredients. Set aside. In another bowl, whisk the wet ingredients. Add the wet ingredients to the dry ingredients and combine until blended.
2. Transfer the batter to 6 silicone muffin cups lightly greased with olive oil. Place muffin cups in the frying basket and Bake for 12 minutes. Serve right away.

Polenta

Servings: 4
Cooking Time: 15 Minutes
Ingredients:

- 1 pound polenta
- ¼ cup flour
- oil for misting or cooking spray

Directions:

1. Cut polenta into ½-inch slices.
2. Dip slices in flour to coat well. Spray both sides with oil or cooking spray.
3. Cook at 390°F for 5minutes. Turn polenta and spray both sides again with oil.
4. Cook 10 more minutes or until brown and crispy.

Chapter 7 Appetizers And Snacks

Shrimp Toasts

Servings: 4

Cooking Time: 8 Minutes

Ingredients:

- ½ pound raw shrimp, peeled and de-veined
- 1 egg (or 2 egg whites)
- 2 scallions, plus more for garnish
- 2 teaspoons grated fresh ginger
- 1 teaspoon soy sauce
- ½ teaspoon toasted sesame oil
- 2 tablespoons chopped fresh cilantro or parsley
- 1 to 2 teaspoons sriracha sauce
- 6 slices thinly-sliced white sandwich bread (Pepperidge Farm®)
- ½ cup sesame seeds
- Thai chili sauce

Directions:

1. Combine the shrimp, egg, scallions, fresh ginger, soy sauce, sesame oil, cilantro (or parsley) and sriracha sauce in a food processor and process into a chunky paste, scraping down the sides of the food processor bowl as necessary.
2. Cut the crusts off the sandwich bread and generously spread the shrimp paste onto each slice of bread. Place the sesame seeds on a plate and invert each shrimp toast into the sesame seeds to coat, pressing down gently. Cut each slice of bread into 4 triangles.
3. Preheat the air fryer to 400°F.
4. Transfer one layer of shrimp toast triangles to the air fryer and air-fry at 400°F for 8 minutes, or until the sesame seeds are toasted on top.
5. Serve warm with a little Thai chili sauce and some sliced scallions as garnish.

Fried Apple Wedges

Servings: 4

Cooking Time: 9 Minutes

Ingredients:

- ¼ cup panko breadcrumbs
- ¼ cup pecans
- 1½ teaspoons cinnamon
- 1½ teaspoons brown sugar
- ¼ cup cornstarch
- 1 egg white
- 2 teaspoons water
- 1 medium apple
- oil for misting or cooking spray

Directions:

1. In a food processor, combine panko, pecans, cinnamon, and brown sugar. Process to make small crumbs.
2. Place cornstarch in a plastic bag or bowl with lid. In a shallow dish, beat together the egg white and water until slightly foamy.
3. Preheat air fryer to 390°F.
4. Cut apple into small wedges. The thickest edge should be no more than ⅜- to ½-inch thick. Cut away the core, but do not peel.
5. Place apple wedges in cornstarch, reseal bag or bowl, and shake to coat.
6. Dip wedges in egg wash, shake off excess, and roll in crumb mixture. Spray with oil.
7. Place apples in air fryer basket in single layer and cook for 5 minutes. Shake basket and break apart any apples that have stuck together. Mist lightly with oil and cook 4 minutes longer, until crispy.

Crispy Chicken Bites With Gorgonzola Sauce

Servings: 4

Cooking Time: 30 Minutes

Ingredients:

- ¼ cup crumbled Gorgonzola cheese
- ¼ cup creamy blue cheese salad dressing
- 1 lb chicken tenders, cut into thirds crosswise
- ½ cup sour cream
- 1 celery stalk, chopped
- 3 tbsp buffalo chicken sauce
- 1 cup panko bread crumbs
- 2 tbsp olive oil

Directions:

1. Preheat air fryer to 350°F. Blend together sour cream, salad dressing, Gorgonzola cheese, and celery in a bowl. Set aside. Combine chicken pieces and Buffalo wing sauce in another bowl until the chicken is coated.

2. In a shallow bowl or pie plate, mix the bread crumbs and olive oil. Dip the chicken into the bread crumb mixture, patting the crumbs to keep them in place. Arrange the chicken in the greased frying basket and Air Fry for 8-9 minutes, shaking once halfway through cooking until the chicken is golden. Serve with the blue cheese sauce.

Fiery Sweet Chicken Wings

Servings: 4

Cooking Time: 30 Minutes

Ingredients:

- 8 chicken wings
- 1 tbsp olive oil
- 3 tbsp brown sugar
- 2 tbsp maple syrup
- ½ cup apple cider vinegar
- ½ tsp Aleppo pepper flakes
- Salt to taste

Directions:

1. Preheat air fryer to 390°F. Toss the wings with olive oil in a bowl. Bake in the air fryer for 20 minutes, shaking the basket twice. While the chicken is cooking, whisk together sugar, maple syrup, vinegar, Aleppo pepper flakes, and salt in a small bowl. Transfer the wings to a baking pan, then pour the sauce over the wings. Toss well to coat. Cook in the air fryer until the wings are glazed, or for another 5 minutes. Serve hot.

Stuffed Mushrooms

Servings: 10

Cooking Time: 8 Minutes

Ingredients:

- 8 ounces white mushroom caps, stems removed
- salt
- 6 fresh mozzarella cheese balls
- ground dried thyme
- ¼ roasted red pepper cut into small pieces (about ½ inch)

Directions:

1. Sprinkle inside of mushroom caps with salt to taste.
2. Cut mozzarella balls in half.
3. Stuff each cap with half a mozzarella cheese ball. Sprinkle very lightly with thyme.
4. Top each mushroom with a small strip of roasted red pepper, lightly pressing it into the cheese.
5. Cook at 390°F for 8minutes or longer if you prefer softer mushrooms.

Green Olive And Mushroom Tapenade

Servings: 1

Cooking Time: 10 Minutes

Ingredients:

- ¾ pound Brown or Baby Bella mushrooms, sliced
- 1½ cups (about ½ pound) Pitted green olives
- 3 tablespoons Olive oil
- 1½ tablespoons Fresh oregano leaves, loosely packed
- ¼ teaspoon Ground black pepper

Directions:

1. Preheat the air fryer to 400°F.
2. When the machine is at temperature, arrange the mushroom slices in as close to an even layer as possible in the basket. They will overlap and even stack on top of each other.
3. Air-fry for 10 minutes, tossing the basket and rearranging the mushrooms every 2 minutes, until shriveled but with still-noticeable moisture.
4. Pour the mushrooms into a food processor. Add the olives, olive oil, oregano leaves, and pepper. Cover and process until grainy, not too much, just not fully smooth for better texture, stopping the machine at least once to scrape down the inside of the canister. Scrape the tapenade into a bowl and serve warm, or cover and refrigerate for up to 4 days. (The tapenade will taste better if it comes back to room temperature before serving.)

Hot Nachos With Chile Salsa

Servings: 4

Cooking Time: 20 Minutes

Ingredients:

- ½ chile de árbol pepper, seeds removed
- 1 tbsp olive oil
- Salt to taste
- 1 shallot, chopped
- 2 garlic cloves
- 1 can diced tomatoes
- 2 tbsp fresh cilantro
- Juice of 1 lime
- ¼ tsp chili-lime seasoning
- 6 corn tortillas

Directions:

1. Add the shallot, garlic, chile de árbol, tomatoes, cilantro, lime juice and salt in a food processor. Pulse until combined and chunky. Pour the salsa into a serving bowl and set aside. Drizzle olive oil on both sides of the tortillas. Stack the tortilla and cut them in half with a sharp knife. Continue to cut into quarters, then cut again so that each tortilla is cut into 8 equal wedges. Season both sides of each wedge with chile-lime seasoning.

2. Preheat air fryer to 400°F. Place the tortilla wedges in the greased frying basket and Air Fry for 4-7 minutes, shaking once until the chips are golden and crisp. Allow to cool slightly and serve with previously prepared salsa.

Herbed Cheese Brittle

Servings: 4

Cooking Time: 5 Minutes

Ingredients:

- ½ cup shredded Parmesan cheese
- ½ cup shredded white cheddar cheese
- 1 tablespoon fresh chopped rosemary
- 1 teaspoon garlic powder
- 1 large egg white

Directions:

1. Preheat the air fryer to 400°F.

2. In a large bowl, mix the cheeses, rosemary, and garlic powder. Mix in the egg white. Then pour the batter into a 7-inch pan (or an air-fryer-compatible pan). Place the pan in the air fryer basket and cook for 4 to 5 minutes, or until the cheese is melted and slightly browned.

3. Remove the pan from the air fryer, and let it cool for 2 minutes. Invert the pan before the cheese brittle completely cools but is semi-hardened to allow it to easily slide out of the pan.

4. Let the pan cool another 5 minutes. Break into pieces and serve.

Homemade Pretzel Bites

Servings: 8
Cooking Time: 6 Minutes

Ingredients:

- 4¾ cups filtered water, divided
- 1 tablespoon butter
- 1 package fast-rising yeast
- ½ teaspoon salt
- 2⅓ cups bread flour
- 2 tablespoons baking soda
- 2 egg whites
- 1 teaspoon kosher salt

Directions:

1. Preheat the air fryer to 370°F.
2. In a large microwave-safe bowl, add ¾ cup of the water. Heat for 40 seconds in the microwave. Remove and whisk in the butter; then mix in the yeast and salt. Let sit 5 minutes.
3. Using a stand mixer with a dough hook attachment, add the yeast liquid and mix in the bread flour ⅓ cup at a time until all the flour is added and a dough is formed.
4. Remove the bowl from the stand; then let the dough rise 1 hour in a warm space, covered with a kitchen towel.
5. After the dough has doubled in size, remove from the bowl and punch down a few times on a lightly floured flat surface.
6. Divide the dough into 4 balls; then roll each ball out into a long, skinny, sticklike shape. Using a sharp knife, cut each dough stick into 6 pieces.
7. Repeat Step 6 for the remaining dough balls until you have about 24 bites formed.
8. Heat the remaining 4 cups of water over the stovetop in a medium pot with the baking soda stirred in.
9. Drop the pretzel bite dough into the hot water and let boil for 60 seconds, remove, and let slightly cool.
10. Lightly brush the top of each bite with the egg whites, and then cover with a pinch of kosher salt.
11. Spray the air fryer basket with olive oil spray and place the pretzel bites on top. Cook for 6 to 8 minutes, or until lightly browned. Remove and keep warm.
12. Repeat until all pretzel bites are cooked.
13. Serve warm.

Roasted Chickpeas

Servings: 1
Cooking Time: 15 Minutes

Ingredients:

- 1 15-ounce can chickpeas, drained
- 2 teaspoons curry powder
- ¼ teaspoon salt
- 1 tablespoon olive oil

Directions:

1. Drain chickpeas thoroughly and spread in a single layer on paper towels. Cover with another paper towel and press gently to remove extra moisture. Don't press too hard or you'll crush the chickpeas.
2. Mix curry powder and salt together.
3. Place chickpeas in a medium bowl and sprinkle with seasonings. Stir well to coat.
4. Add olive oil and stir again to distribute oil.
5. Cook at 390°F for 15minutes, stopping to shake basket about halfway through cooking time.
6. Cool completely and store in airtight container.

Dijon Chicken Wings

Servings: 6

Cooking Time: 60 Minutes

Ingredients:

- 2 lb chicken wings, split at the joint
- 1 tbsp water
- 1 tbs salt
- 1 tsp black pepper
- 1 tsp red chili powder
- 1 tbsp butter, melted
- 1 tbsp Dijon mustard
- 2 tbsp yellow mustard
- ¼ cup honey
- 1 tsp apple cider vinegar
- Salt to taste

Directions:

1. Preheat air fryer at 250°F. Pour water in the bottom of the frying basket to ensure minimum smoke from fat drippings. Sprinkle the chicken wings with salt, pepper, and red chili powder. Place chicken wings in the greased frying basket and Air Fry for 12 minutes, tossing once. Whisk the remaining ingredients in a bowl. Add in chicken wings and toss to coat. Serve immediately.

Maple Loaded Sweet Potatoes

Servings: 4

Cooking Time: 45 Minutes

Ingredients:

- 4 sweet potatoes
- 2 tbsp butter
- 2 tbsp maple syrup
- 1 tsp cinnamon
- 1 tsp lemon zest
- ½ tsp vanilla extract

Directions:

1. Preheat air fryer to 390°F. Poke three holes on the top of each of the sweet potatoes using a fork. Arrange in air fryer and Bake for 40 minutes. Remove and let cool for 5 minutes. While the sweet potatoes cool, melt butter and maple syrup together in the microwave for 15-20 seconds. Remove from microwave and stir in cinnamon, lemon zest, and vanilla. When the sweet potatoes are cool, cut open and drizzle the cinnamon butter mixture over each and serve immediately.

Avocado Fries

Servings: 8

Cooking Time: 8 Minutes

Ingredients:

- 2 medium avocados, firm but ripe
- 1 large egg
- ½ teaspoon garlic powder
- ¼ teaspoon cayenne pepper
- ¼ teaspoon salt
- ¾ cup almond flour
- ½ cup finely grated Parmesan cheese
- ½ cup gluten-free breadcrumbs

Directions:

1. Preheat the air fryer to 370°F.
2. Rinse the outside of the avocado with water. Slice the avocado in half, slice it in half again, and then slice it in half once more to get 8 slices. Remove the outer skin. Repeat for the other avocado. Set the avocado slices aside.
3. In a small bowl, whisk the egg, garlic powder, cayenne pepper, and salt in a small bowl. Set aside.
4. In a separate bowl, pour the almond flour.
5. In a third bowl, mix the Parmesan cheese and breadcrumbs.
6. Carefully roll the avocado slices in the almond flour, then dip them in the egg wash, and coat them in the cheese and breadcrumb topping. Repeat until all 16 fries are coated.
7. Liberally spray the air fryer basket with olive oil spray and place the avocado fries into the basket, leaving a little space around the sides between fries. Depending on the size of your air fryer, you may need to cook these in batches.
8. Cook fries for 8 minutes, or until the outer coating turns light brown.
9. Carefully remove, repeat with remaining slices, and then serve warm.

Spicy Pearl Onion Dip

Servings: 4

Cooking Time: 20 Minutes+chilling Time

Ingredients:

- 2 cups peeled pearl onions
- 3 garlic cloves
- 3 tbsp olive oil
- Salt and pepper to taste
- 1 cup Greek yogurt
- ¼ tsp Worcestershire sauce
- 1 tbsp lemon juice
- ⅛ tsp red pepper flakes
- 1 tbsp chives, chopped

Directions:

1. Preheat air fryer to 360°F. Place the onions, garlic, and 2 tbsp of olive oil in a bowl and combine until the onions are well coated. Pour the mixture into the frying basket and Roast for 11-13 minutes. Transfer the garlic and onions to your food processor. Pulse the vegetables several times until the onions are minced but still have some chunks.
2. Combine the garlic and onions and the remaining olive oil, along with the salt, yogurt, Worcestershire sauce, lemon juice, black pepper, chives and red pepper flakes in a bowl. Cover and chill for at least 1 hour. Serve with toasted bread if desired.

Eggplant Fries

Servings: 18
Cooking Time: 10 Minutes

Ingredients:

- ¾ cup All-purpose flour or tapioca flour
- 1 Large egg(s), well beaten
- 1 cup Seasoned Italian-style dried bread crumbs (gluten-free, if a concern)
- 3 tablespoons (about ½ ounce) Finely grated Asiago or Parmesan cheese
- 3 Peeled ½-inch-thick eggplant slices (each about 3 inches in diameter)
- Olive oil spray

Directions:

1. Preheat the air fryer to 375°F (or 380°F or 390°F, if one of these is the closest setting).

2. Set up and fill three shallow soup plates or small pie plates on your counter: one for the flour, one for the egg(s), and one for the bread crumbs mixed with the cheese until well combined.

3. Cut each eggplant slice into six ½-inch-wide strips or sticks. Dip one strip in the flour, coating it well on all sides. Gently shake off the excess flour, then dip the strip in the beaten egg(s) to coat it without losing the flour. Let any excess egg slip back into the rest, then roll the strip in the bread-crumb mixture to coat evenly on all sides, even the ends. Set the strips aside on a cutting board and continue dipping and coating the remaining strips as you did the first one.

4. Generously coat the strips with olive oil spray on all sides. Set them in the basket in one layer and air-fry undisturbed for 10 minutes, or until golden brown and crisp. If the machine is at 390°F, the strips may be done in 8 minutes.

5. Remove the basket from the machine and cool for a couple of minutes. Then use kitchen tongs to transfer the eggplant fries to a wire rack to cool for only a minute or two more before serving.

Garlic Breadsticks

Servings: 12
Cooking Time: 7 Minutes

Ingredients:

- 1½ tablespoons Olive oil
- 1½ teaspoons Minced garlic
- ¼ teaspoon Table salt
- ¼ teaspoon Ground black pepper
- 6 ounces Purchased pizza dough (vegan dough, if that's a concern)

Directions:

1. Preheat the air fryer to 400°F. Mix the oil, garlic, salt, and pepper in a small bowl.

2. Divide the pizza dough into 4 balls for a small air fryer, 6 for a medium machine, or 8 for a large, each ball about the size of a walnut in its shell. (Each should weigh 1 ounce, if you want to drag out a scale and get obsessive.) Roll each ball into a 5-inch-long stick under your clean palms on a clean, dry work surface. Brush the sticks with the oil mixture.

3. When the machine is at temperature, place the prepared dough sticks in the basket, leaving a 1-inch space between them. Air-fry undisturbed for 7 minutes, or until puffed, golden, and set to the touch.

4. Use kitchen tongs to gently transfer the breadsticks to a wire rack and repeat step 3 with the remaining dough sticks.

Indian Cauliflower Tikka Bites

Servings: 6

Cooking Time: 20 Minutes

Ingredients:

- 1 cup plain Greek yogurt
- 1 teaspoon fresh ginger
- 1 teaspoon minced garlic
- 1 teaspoon vindaloo
- ½ teaspoon cardamom
- ½ teaspoon paprika
- ½ teaspoon turmeric powder
- ½ teaspoon cumin powder
- 1 large head of cauliflower, washed and cut into medium-size florets
- ½ cup panko breadcrumbs
- 1 lemon, quartered

Directions:

1. Preheat the air fryer to 350°F.

2. In a large bowl, mix the yogurt, ginger, garlic, vindaloo, cardamom, paprika, turmeric, and cumin. Add the cauliflower florets to the bowl, and coat them with the yogurt.

3. Remove the cauliflower florets from the bowl and place them on a baking sheet. Sprinkle the panko breadcrumbs over the top. Place the cauliflower bites into the air fryer basket, leaving space between the florets. Depending on the size of your air fryer, you may need to make more than one batch.

4. Cook the cauliflower for 10 minutes, shake the basket, and continue cooking another 10 minutes (or until the florets are lightly browned).

5. Remove from the air fryer and keep warm. Continue to cook until all the florets are done.

6. Before serving, lightly squeeze lemon over the top. Serve warm.

Classic Potato Chips

Servings: 4

Cooking Time: 8 Minutes

Ingredients:

- 2 medium russet potatoes, washed
- 2 cups filtered water
- 1 tablespoon avocado oil
- ½ teaspoon salt

Directions:

1. Using a mandolin, slice the potatoes into ⅛-inch-thick pieces.

2. Pour the water into a large bowl. Place the potatoes in the bowl and soak for at least 30 minutes.

3. Preheat the air fryer to 350°F.

4. Drain the water and pat the potatoes dry with a paper towel or kitchen cloth. Toss with avocado oil and salt. Liberally spray the air fryer basket with olive oil mist.

5. Set the potatoes inside the air fryer basket, separating them so they're not on top of each other. Cook for 5 minutes, shake the basket, and cook another 5 minutes, or until browned.

6. Remove and let cool a few minutes prior to serving. Repeat until all the chips are cooked.

Granola Three Ways

Servings: 4

Cooking Time: 10 Minutes

Ingredients:

- Nantucket Granola
- ¼ cup maple syrup
- ¼ cup dark brown sugar
- 1 tablespoon butter
- 1 teaspoon vanilla extract
- 1 cup rolled oats
- ½ cup dried cranberries
- ½ cup walnuts, chopped
- ¼ cup pumpkin seeds
- ¼ cup shredded coconut
- Blueberry Delight
- ¼ cup honey
- ¼ cup light brown sugar
- 1 tablespoon butter
- 1 teaspoon lemon extract
- 1 cup rolled oats
- ½ cup sliced almonds
- ½ cup dried blueberries
- ¼ cup pumpkin seeds
- ¼ cup sunflower seeds
- Cherry Black Forest Mix
- ¼ cup honey
- ¼ cup light brown sugar
- 1 tablespoon butter
- 1 teaspoon almond extract
- 1 cup rolled oats
- ½ cup sliced almonds
- ½ cup dried cherries
- ¼ cup shredded coconut
- ¼ cup dark chocolate chips
- oil for misting or cooking spray

Directions:

1. Combine the syrup or honey, brown sugar, and butter in a small saucepan or microwave-safe bowl. Heat and stir just until butter melts and sugar dissolves. Stir in the extract.

2. Place all other dry ingredients in a large bowl. (For the Cherry Black Forest Mix, don't add the chocolate chips yet.)

3. Pour melted butter mixture over dry ingredients and stir until oat mixture is well coated.

4. Lightly spray a baking pan with oil or cooking spray.

5. Pour granola into pan and cook at 390°F for 5minutes. Stir. Continue cooking for 5minutes, stirring every minute or two, until golden brown. Watch closely. Once the mixture begins to brown, it will cook quickly.

6. Remove granola from pan and spread on wax paper. It will become crispier as it cools.

7. For the Cherry Black Forest Mix, stir in chocolate chips after granola has cooled completely.

8. Store in an airtight container.

Home-style Taro Chips

Servings: 2
Cooking Time: 20 Minutes
Ingredients:

- 1 tbsp olive oil
- 1 cup thinly sliced taro
- Salt to taste
- ½ cup hummus

Directions:

1. Preheat air fryer to 325°F. Put the sliced taro in the greased frying basket, spread the pieces out, and drizzle with olive oil. Air Fry for 10-12 minutes, shaking the basket twice. Sprinkle with salt and serve with hummus.

Chapter 8 Sandwiches And Burgers Recipes

Thai-style Pork Sliders

Servings: 4
Cooking Time: 15 Minutes
Ingredients:

- 11 ounces Ground pork
- 2½ tablespoons Very thinly sliced scallions, white and green parts
- 4 teaspoons Minced peeled fresh ginger
- 2½ teaspoons Fish sauce (gluten-free, if a concern)
- 2 teaspoons Thai curry paste (see the headnote; gluten-free, if a concern)
- 2 teaspoons Light brown sugar
- ¾ teaspoon Ground black pepper
- 4 Slider buns (gluten-free, if a concern)

Directions:

1. Preheat the air fryer to 375°F .
2. Gently mix the pork, scallions, ginger, fish sauce, curry paste, brown sugar, and black pepper in a bowl until well combined. With clean, wet hands, form about ⅓ cup of the pork mixture into a slider about 2½ inches in diameter. Repeat until you use up all the meat—3 sliders for the small batch, 4 for the medium, and 6 for the large. (Keep wetting your hands to help the patties adhere.)
3. When the machine is at temperature, set the sliders in the basket in one layer. Air-fry undisturbed for 14 minutes, or until the sliders are golden brown and caramelized at their edges and an instant-read meat thermometer inserted into the center of a slider registers 160°F.
4. Use a nonstick-safe spatula, and perhaps a flatware fork for balance, to transfer the sliders to a cutting board. Set the buns cut side down in the basket in one layer (working in batches as necessary) and air-fry undisturbed for 1 minute, to toast a bit and warm up. Serve the sliders warm in the buns.

Chicken Apple Brie Melt

Servings: 3

Cooking Time: 13 Minutes

Ingredients:

- 3 5- to 6-ounce boneless skinless chicken breasts
- Vegetable oil spray
- 1½ teaspoons Dried herbes de Provence
- 3 ounces Brie, rind removed, thinly sliced
- 6 Thin cored apple slices
- 3 French rolls (gluten-free, if a concern)
- 2 tablespoons Dijon mustard (gluten-free, if a concern)

Directions:

1. Preheat the air fryer to 375°F .

2. Lightly coat all sides of the chicken breasts with vegetable oil spray. Sprinkle the breasts evenly with the herbes de Provence.

3. When the machine is at temperature, set the breasts in the basket and air-fry undisturbed for 10 minutes.

4. Top the chicken breasts with the apple slices, then the cheese. Air-fry undisturbed for 2 minutes, or until the cheese is melty and bubbling.

5. Use a nonstick-safe spatula and kitchen tongs, for balance, to transfer the breasts to a cutting board. Set the rolls in the basket and air-fry for 1 minute to warm through. (Putting them in the machine without splitting them keeps the insides very soft while the outside gets a little crunchy.)

6. Transfer the rolls to the cutting board. Split them open lengthwise, then spread 1 teaspoon mustard on each cut side. Set a prepared chicken breast on the bottom of a roll and close with its top, repeating as necessary to make additional sandwiches. Serve warm.

Chili Cheese Dogs

Servings: 3

Cooking Time: 12 Minutes

Ingredients:

- ¾ pound Lean ground beef
- 1½ tablespoons Chile powder
- 1 cup plus 2 tablespoons Jarred sofrito
- 3 Hot dogs (gluten-free, if a concern)
- 3 Hot dog buns (gluten-free, if a concern), split open lengthwise
- 3 tablespoons Finely chopped scallion
- 9 tablespoons (a little more than 2 ounces) Shredded Cheddar cheese

Directions:

1. Crumble the ground beef into a medium or large saucepan set over medium heat. Brown well, stirring often to break up the clumps. Add the chile powder and cook for 30 seconds, stirring the whole time. Stir in the sofrito and bring to a simmer. Reduce the heat to low and simmer, stirring occasionally, for 5 minutes. Keep warm.

2. Preheat the air fryer to 400°F.

3. When the machine is at temperature, put the hot dogs in the basket and air-fry undisturbed for 10 minutes, or until the hot dogs are bubbling and blistered, even a little crisp.

4. Use kitchen tongs to put the hot dogs in the buns. Top each with a ½ cup of the ground beef mixture, 1 tablespoon of the minced scallion, and 3 tablespoons of the cheese. (The scallion should go under the cheese so it superheats and wilts a bit.) Set the filled hot dog buns in the basket and air-fry undisturbed for 2 minutes, or until the cheese has melted.

5. Remove the basket from the machine. Cool the chili cheese dogs in the basket for 5 minutes before serving.

Thanksgiving Turkey Sandwiches

Servings: 3

Cooking Time: 10 Minutes

Ingredients:

- 1½ cups Herb-seasoned stuffing mix (not cornbread-style; gluten-free, if a concern)
- 1 Large egg white(s)
- 2 tablespoons Water
- 3 5- to 6-ounce turkey breast cutlets
- Vegetable oil spray
- 4½ tablespoons Purchased cranberry sauce, preferably whole berry
- ⅛ teaspoon Ground cinnamon
- ⅛ teaspoon Ground dried ginger
- 4½ tablespoons Regular, low-fat, or fat-free mayonnaise (gluten-free, if a concern)
- 6 tablespoons Shredded Brussels sprouts
- 3 Kaiser rolls (gluten-free, if a concern), split open

Directions:

1. Preheat the air fryer to 375°F .

2. Put the stuffing mix in a heavy zip-closed bag, seal it, lay it flat on your counter, and roll a rolling pin over the bag to crush the stuffing mix to the consistency of rough sand. (Or you can pulse the stuffing mix to the desired consistency in a food processor.)

3. Set up and fill two shallow soup plates or small pie plates on your counter: one for the egg white(s), whisked with the water until foamy; and one for the ground stuffing mix.

4. Dip a cutlet in the egg white mixture, coating both sides and letting any excess egg white slip back into the rest. Set the cutlet in the ground stuffing mix and coat it evenly on both sides, pressing gently to coat well on both sides. Lightly coat the cutlet on both sides with vegetable oil spray, set it aside, and continue dipping and coating the remaining cutlets in the same way.

5. Set the cutlets in the basket and air-fry undisturbed for 10 minutes, or until crisp and brown. Use kitchen tongs to transfer the cutlets to a wire rack to cool for a few minutes.

6. Meanwhile, stir the cranberry sauce with the cinnamon and ginger in a small bowl. Mix the shredded Brussels sprouts and mayonnaise in a second bowl until the vegetable is evenly coated.

7. Build the sandwiches by spreading about 1½ tablespoons of the cranberry mixture on the cut side of the bottom half of each roll. Set a cutlet on top, then spread about 3 tablespoons of the Brussels sprouts mixture evenly over the cutlet. Set the other half of the roll on top and serve warm.

Black Bean Veggie Burgers

Servings: 3

Cooking Time: 10 Minutes

Ingredients:

- 1 cup Drained and rinsed canned black beans
- ⅓ cup Pecan pieces
- ⅓ cup Rolled oats (not quick-cooking or steel-cut; gluten-free, if a concern)
- 2 tablespoons (or 1 small egg) Pasteurized egg substitute, such as Egg Beaters (gluten-free, if a concern)
- 2 teaspoons Red ketchup-like chili sauce, such as Heinz
- ¼ teaspoon Ground cumin
- ¼ teaspoon Dried oregano
- ¼ teaspoon Table salt
- ¼ teaspoon Ground black pepper
- Olive oil
- Olive oil spray

Directions:

1. Preheat the air fryer to 400°F.

2. Put the beans, pecans, oats, egg substitute or egg, chili sauce, cumin, oregano, salt, and pepper in a food processor. Cover and process to a coarse paste that will hold its shape like sugar-cookie dough, adding olive oil in 1-teaspoon increments to get the mixture to blend smoothly. The amount of olive oil is actually dependent on the internal moisture content of the beans and the oats. Figure on about 1 tablespoon (three 1-teaspoon additions) for the smaller batch, with proportional increases for the other batches. A little too much olive oil can't hurt, but a dry paste will fall apart as it cooks and a far-too-wet paste will stick to the basket.

3. Scrape down and remove the blade. Using clean, wet hands, form the paste into two 4-inch patties for the small batch, three 4-inch patties for the medium, or four 4-inch patties for the large batch, setting them one by one on a cutting board. Generously coat both sides of the patties with olive oil spray.

4. Set them in the basket in one layer. Air-fry undisturbed for 10 minutes, or until lightly browned and crisp at the edges.

5. Use a nonstick-safe spatula, and perhaps a flatware fork for balance, to transfer the burgers to a wire rack. Cool for 5 minutes before serving.

Crunchy Falafel Balls

Servings: 8

Cooking Time: 16 Minutes

Ingredients:

- 2½ cups Drained and rinsed canned chickpeas
- ¼ cup Olive oil
- 3 tablespoons All-purpose flour
- 1½ teaspoons Dried oregano
- 1½ teaspoons Dried sage leaves
- 1½ teaspoons Dried thyme
- ¾ teaspoon Table salt
- Olive oil spray

Directions:

1. Preheat the air fryer to 400°F.

2. Place the chickpeas, olive oil, flour, oregano, sage, thyme, and salt in a food processor. Cover and process into a paste, stopping the machine at least once to scrape down the inside of the canister.

3. Scrape down and remove the blade. Using clean, wet hands, form 2 tablespoons of the paste into a ball, then continue making 9 more balls for a small batch, 15 more for a medium one, and 19 more for a large batch. Generously coat the balls in olive oil spray.

4. Set the balls in the basket in one layer with a little space between them and air-fry undisturbed for 16 minutes, or until well browned and crisp.

5. Dump the contents of the basket onto a wire rack. Cool for 5 minutes before serving.

Chicken Spiedies

Servings: 3
Cooking Time: 12 Minutes

Ingredients:

- 1¼ pounds Boneless skinless chicken thighs, trimmed of any fat blobs and cut into 2-inch pieces
- 3 tablespoons Red wine vinegar
- 2 tablespoons Olive oil
- 2 tablespoons Minced fresh mint leaves
- 2 tablespoons Minced fresh parsley leaves
- 2 teaspoons Minced fresh dill fronds
- ¾ teaspoon Fennel seeds
- ¾ teaspoon Table salt
- Up to a ¼ teaspoon Red pepper flakes
- 3 Long soft rolls, such as hero, hoagie, or Italian sub rolls (gluten-free, if a concern), split open lengthwise
- 4½ tablespoons Regular or low-fat mayonnaise (not fat-free; gluten-free, if a concern)
- 1½ tablespoons Distilled white vinegar
- 1½ teaspoons Ground black pepper

Directions:

1. Mix the chicken, vinegar, oil, mint, parsley, dill, fennel seeds, salt, and red pepper flakes in a zip-closed plastic bag. Seal, gently massage the marinade ingredients into the meat, and refrigerate for at least 2 hours or up to 6 hours. (Longer than that and the meat can turn rubbery.)

2. Set the plastic bag out on the counter (to make the contents a little less frigid). Preheat the air fryer to 400°F.

3. When the machine is at temperature, use kitchen tongs to set the chicken thighs in the basket (discard any remaining marinade) and air-fry undisturbed for 6 minutes. Turn the thighs over and continue air-frying undisturbed for 6 minutes more, until well browned, cooked through, and even a little crunchy.

4. Dump the contents of the basket onto a wire rack and cool for 2 or 3 minutes. Divide the chicken evenly between the rolls. Whisk the mayonnaise, vinegar, and black pepper in a small bowl until smooth. Drizzle this sauce over the chicken pieces in the rolls.

Inside Out Cheeseburgers

Servings: 2
Cooking Time: 20 Minutes

Ingredients:

- ¾ pound lean ground beef
- 3 tablespoons minced onion
- 4 teaspoons ketchup
- 2 teaspoons yellow mustard
- salt and freshly ground black pepper
- 4 slices of Cheddar cheese, broken into smaller pieces
- 8 hamburger dill pickle chips

Directions:

1. Combine the ground beef, minced onion, ketchup, mustard, salt and pepper in a large bowl. Mix well to thoroughly combine the ingredients. Divide the meat into four equal portions.

2. To make the stuffed burgers, flatten each portion of meat into a thin patty. Place 4 pickle chips and half of the cheese onto the center of two of the patties, leaving a rim around the edge of the patty exposed. Place the remaining two patties on top of the first and press the meat together firmly, sealing the edges tightly. With the burgers on a flat surface, press the sides of the burger with the palm of your hand to create a straight edge. This will help keep the stuffing inside the burger while it cooks.

3. Preheat the air fryer to 370°F.

4. Place the burgers inside the air fryer basket and air-fry for 20 minutes, flipping the burgers over halfway through the cooking time.

5. Serve the cheeseburgers on buns with lettuce and tomato.

Provolone Stuffed Meatballs

Servings: 4
Cooking Time: 12 Minutes
Ingredients:

- 1 tablespoon olive oil
- 1 small onion, very finely chopped
- 1 to 2 cloves garlic, minced
- ¾ pound ground beef
- ¾ pound ground pork
- ¾ cup breadcrumbs
- ¼ cup grated Parmesan cheese
- ¼ cup finely chopped fresh parsley (or 1 tablespoon dried parsley)
- ½ teaspoon dried oregano
- 1½ teaspoons salt
- freshly ground black pepper
- 2 eggs, lightly beaten
- 5 ounces sharp or aged provolone cheese, cut into 1-inch cubes

Directions:

1. Preheat a skillet over medium-high heat. Add the oil and cook the onion and garlic until tender, but not browned.
2. Transfer the onion and garlic to a large bowl and add the beef, pork, breadcrumbs, Parmesan cheese, parsley, oregano, salt, pepper and eggs. Mix well until all the ingredients are combined. Divide the mixture into 12 evenly sized balls. Make one meatball at a time, by pressing a hole in the meatball mixture with your finger and pushing a piece of provolone cheese into the hole. Mold the meat back into a ball, enclosing the cheese.
3. Preheat the air fryer to 380°F.
4. Working in two batches, transfer six of the meatballs to the air fryer basket and air-fry for 12 minutes, shaking the basket and turning the meatballs a couple of times during the cooking process. Repeat with the remaining six meatballs. You can pop the first batch of meatballs into the air fryer for the last two minutes of cooking to re-heat them. Serve warm.

Chicken Saltimbocca Sandwiches

Servings: 3
Cooking Time: 11 Minutes
Ingredients:

- 3 5- to 6-ounce boneless skinless chicken breasts
- 6 Thin prosciutto slices
- 6 Provolone cheese slices
- 3 Long soft rolls, such as hero, hoagie, or Italian sub rolls (gluten-free, if a concern), split open lengthwise
- 3 tablespoons Pesto, purchased or homemade (see the headnote)

Directions:

1. Preheat the air fryer to 400°F.
2. Wrap each chicken breast with 2 prosciutto slices, spiraling the prosciutto around the breast and overlapping the slices a bit to cover the breast. The prosciutto will stick to the chicken more readily than bacon does.
3. When the machine is at temperature, set the wrapped chicken breasts in the basket and air-fry undisturbed for 10 minutes, or until the prosciutto is frizzled and the chicken is cooked through.
4. Overlap 2 cheese slices on each breast. Air-fry undisturbed for 1 minute, or until melted. Take the basket out of the machine.
5. Smear the insides of the rolls with the pesto, then use kitchen tongs to put a wrapped and cheesy chicken breast in each roll.

Mexican Cheeseburgers

Servings: 4
Cooking Time: 22 Minutes

Ingredients:

- 1¼ pounds ground beef
- ¼ cup finely chopped onion
- ½ cup crushed yellow corn tortilla chips
- 1 (1.25-ounce) packet taco seasoning
- ¼ cup canned diced green chilies
- 1 egg, lightly beaten
- 4 ounces pepper jack cheese, grated
- 4 (12-inch) flour tortillas
- shredded lettuce, sour cream, guacamole, salsa (for topping)

Directions:

1. Combine the ground beef, minced onion, crushed tortilla chips, taco seasoning, green chilies, and egg in a large bowl. Mix thoroughly until combined – your hands are good tools for this. Divide the meat into four equal portions and shape each portion into an oval-shaped burger.

2. Preheat the air fryer to 370°F.

3. Air-fry the burgers for 18 minutes, turning them over halfway through the cooking time. Divide the cheese between the burgers, lower fryer to 340°F and air-fry for an additional 4 minutes to melt the cheese. (This will give you a burger that is medium-well. If you prefer your cheeseburger medium-rare, shorten the cooking time to about 15 minutes and then add the cheese and proceed with the recipe.)

4. While the burgers are cooking, warm the tortillas wrapped in aluminum foil in a 350°F oven, or in a skillet with a little oil over medium-high heat for a couple of minutes. Keep the tortillas warm until the burgers are ready.

5. To assemble the burgers, spread sour cream over three quarters of the tortillas and top each with some shredded lettuce and salsa. Place the Mexican cheeseburgers on the lettuce and top with guacamole. Fold the tortillas around the burger, starting with the bottom and then folding the sides in over the top. (A little sour cream can help hold the seam of the tortilla together.) Serve immediately.

Sausage And Pepper Heros

Servings: 3
Cooking Time: 11 Minutes

Ingredients:

- 3 links (about 9 ounces total) Sweet Italian sausages (gluten-free, if a concern)
- 1½ Medium red or green bell pepper(s), stemmed, cored, and cut into ½-inch-wide strips
- 1 medium Yellow or white onion(s), peeled, halved, and sliced into thin half-moons
- 3 Long soft rolls, such as hero, hoagie, or Italian sub rolls (gluten-free, if a concern), split open lengthwise
- For garnishing Balsamic vinegar
- For garnishing Fresh basil leaves

Directions:

1. Preheat the air fryer to 400°F.

2. When the machine is at temperature, set the sausage links in the basket in one layer and air-fry undisturbed for 5 minutes.

3. Add the pepper strips and onions. Continue air-frying, tossing and rearranging everything about once every minute, for 5 minutes, or until the sausages are browned and an instant-read meat thermometer inserted into one of the links registers 160°F.

4. Use a nonstick-safe spatula and kitchen tongs to transfer the sausages and vegetables to a cutting board. Set the rolls cut side down in the basket in one layer (working in batches as necessary) and air-fry undisturbed for 1 minute, to toast the rolls a bit and warm them up. Set 1 sausage with some pepper strips and onions in each warm roll, sprinkle balsamic vinegar over the sandwich fillings, and garnish with basil leaves.

Chicken Club Sandwiches

Servings: 3

Cooking Time: 15 Minutes

Ingredients:

- 3 5- to 6-ounce boneless skinless chicken breasts
- 6 Thick-cut bacon strips (gluten-free, if a concern)
- 3 Long soft rolls, such as hero, hoagie, or Italian sub rolls (gluten-free, if a concern)
- 3 tablespoons Regular, low-fat, or fat-free mayonnaise (gluten-free, if a concern)
- 3 Lettuce leaves, preferably romaine or iceberg
- 6 ¼-inch-thick tomato slices

Directions:

1. Preheat the air fryer to 375°F .
2. Wrap each chicken breast with 2 strips of bacon, spiraling the bacon around the meat, slightly overlapping the strips on each revolution. Start the second strip of bacon farther down the breast but on a line with the start of the first strip so they both end at a lined-up point on the chicken breast.
3. When the machine is at temperature, set the wrapped breasts bacon-seam side down in the basket with space between them. Air-fry undisturbed for 12 minutes, until the bacon is browned, crisp, and cooked through and an instant-read meat thermometer inserted into the center of a breast registers 165°F. You may need to add 2 minutes in the air fryer if the temperature is at 360°F.
4. Use kitchen tongs to transfer the breasts to a wire rack. Split the rolls open lengthwise and set them cut side down in the basket. Air-fry for 1 minute, or until warmed through.
5. Use kitchen tongs to transfer the rolls to a cutting board. Spread 1 tablespoon mayonnaise on the cut side of one half of each roll. Top with a chicken breast, lettuce leaf, and tomato slice. Serve warm.

Salmon Burgers

Servings: 3

Cooking Time: 8 Minutes

Ingredients:

- 1 pound 2 ounces Skinless salmon fillet, preferably fattier Atlantic salmon
- 1½ tablespoons Minced chives or the green part of a scallion
- ½ cup Plain panko bread crumbs (gluten-free, if a concern)
- 1½ teaspoons Dijon mustard (gluten-free, if a concern)
- 1½ teaspoons Drained and rinsed capers, minced
- 1½ teaspoons Lemon juice
- ¼ teaspoon Table salt
- ¼ teaspoon Ground black pepper
- Vegetable oil spray

Directions:

1. Preheat the air fryer to 375°F .
2. Cut the salmon into pieces that will fit in a food processor. Cover and pulse until coarsely chopped. Add the chives and pulse to combine, until the fish is ground but not a paste. Scrape down and remove the blade. Scrape the salmon mixture into a bowl. Add the bread crumbs, mustard, capers, lemon juice, salt, and pepper. Stir gently until well combined.
3. Use clean and dry hands to form the mixture into two 5-inch patties for a small batch, three 5-inch patties for a medium batch, or four 5-inch patties for a large one.
4. Coat both sides of each patty with vegetable oil spray. Set them in the basket in one layer and air-fry undisturbed for 8 minutes, or until browned and an instant-read meat thermometer inserted into the center of a burger registers 145°F.
5. Use a nonstick-safe spatula, and perhaps a flatware fork for balance, to transfer the burgers to a wire rack. Cool for 2 or 3 minutes before serving.

Chicken Gyros

Servings: 4

Cooking Time: 14 Minutes

Ingredients:

- 4 4- to 5-ounce boneless skinless chicken thighs, trimmed of any fat blobs
- 2 tablespoons Lemon juice
- 2 tablespoons Red wine vinegar
- 2 tablespoons Olive oil
- 2 teaspoons Dried oregano
- 2 teaspoons Minced garlic
- 1 teaspoon Table salt
- 1 teaspoon Ground black pepper
- 4 Pita pockets (gluten-free, if a concern)
- ½ cup Chopped tomatoes
- ½ cup Bottled regular, low-fat, or fat-free ranch dressing (gluten-free, if a concern)

Directions:

1. Mix the thighs, lemon juice, vinegar, oil, oregano, garlic, salt, and pepper in a zip-closed bag. Seal, gently massage the marinade into the meat through the plastic, and refrigerate for at least 2 hours or up to 6 hours. (Longer than that and the meat can turn rubbery.)

2. Set the plastic bag out on the counter (to make the contents a little less frigid). Preheat the air fryer to 375°F .

3. When the machine is at temperature, use kitchen tongs to place the thighs in the basket in one layer. Discard the marinade. Air-fry the chicken thighs undisturbed for 12 minutes, or until browned and an instant-read meat thermometer inserted into the thickest part of one thigh registers 165°F. You may need to air-fry the chicken 2 minutes longer if the machine's temperature is 360°F.

4. Use kitchen tongs to transfer the thighs to a cutting board. Cool for 5 minutes, then set one thigh in each of the pita pockets. Top each with 2 tablespoons chopped tomatoes and 2 tablespoons dressing. Serve warm.

Lamb Burgers

Servings: 3

Cooking Time: 17 Minutes

Ingredients:

- 1 pound 2 ounces Ground lamb
- 3 tablespoons Crumbled feta
- 1 teaspoon Minced garlic
- 1 teaspoon Tomato paste
- ¾ teaspoon Ground coriander
- ¾ teaspoon Ground dried ginger
- Up to ⅛ teaspoon Cayenne
- Up to a ⅛ teaspoon Table salt (optional)
- 3 Kaiser rolls or hamburger buns (gluten-free, if a concern), split open

Directions:

1. Preheat the air fryer to 375°F .

2. Gently mix the ground lamb, feta, garlic, tomato paste, coriander, ginger, cayenne, and salt (if using) in a bowl until well combined, trying to keep the bits of cheese intact. Form this mixture into two 5-inch patties for the small batch, three 5-inch patties for the medium, or four 5-inch patties for the large.

3. Set the patties in the basket in one layer and air-fry undisturbed for 16 minutes, or until an instant-read meat thermometer inserted into one burger registers 160°F. (The cheese is not an issue with the temperature probe in this recipe as it was for the Inside-Out Cheeseburgers, because the feta is so well mixed into the ground meat.)

4. Use a nonstick-safe spatula, and perhaps a flatware fork for balance, to transfer the burgers to a cutting board. Set the buns cut side down in the basket in one layer (working in batches as necessary) and air-fry undisturbed for 1 minute, to toast a bit and warm up. Serve the burgers warm in the buns.

Asian Glazed Meatballs

Servings: 4

Cooking Time: 10 Minutes

Ingredients:

- 1 large shallot, finely chopped
- 2 cloves garlic, minced
- 1 tablespoon grated fresh ginger
- 2 teaspoons fresh thyme, finely chopped
- 1½ cups brown mushrooms, very finely chopped (a food processor works well here)
- 2 tablespoons soy sauce
- freshly ground black pepper
- 1 pound ground beef
- ½ pound ground pork
- 3 egg yolks
- 1 cup Thai sweet chili sauce (spring roll sauce)
- ¼ cup toasted sesame seeds
- 2 scallions, sliced

Directions:

1. Combine the shallot, garlic, ginger, thyme, mushrooms, soy sauce, freshly ground black pepper, ground beef and pork, and egg yolks in a bowl and mix the ingredients together. Gently shape the mixture into 24 balls, about the size of a golf ball.

2. Preheat the air fryer to 380°F.

3. Working in batches, air-fry the meatballs for 8 minutes, turning the meatballs over halfway through the cooking time. Drizzle some of the Thai sweet chili sauce on top of each meatball and return the basket to the air fryer, air-frying for another 2 minutes. Reserve the remaining Thai sweet chili sauce for serving.

4. As soon as the meatballs are done, sprinkle with toasted sesame seeds and transfer them to a serving platter. Scatter the scallions around and serve warm.

Philly Cheesesteak Sandwiches

Servings: 3

Cooking Time: 9 Minutes

Ingredients:

- ¾ pound Shaved beef
- 1 tablespoon Worcestershire sauce (gluten-free, if a concern)
- ¼ teaspoon Garlic powder
- ¼ teaspoon Mild paprika
- 6 tablespoons (1½ ounces) Frozen bell pepper strips (do not thaw)
- 2 slices, broken into rings Very thin yellow or white medium onion slice(s)
- 6 ounces (6 to 8 slices) Provolone cheese slices
- 3 Long soft rolls such as hero, hoagie, or Italian sub rolls, or hot dog buns (gluten-free, if a concern), split open lengthwise

Directions:

1. Preheat the air fryer to 400°F.

2. When the machine is at temperature, spread the shaved beef in the basket, leaving a ½-inch perimeter around the meat for good air flow. Sprinkle the meat with the Worcestershire sauce, paprika, and garlic powder. Spread the peppers and onions on top of the meat.

3. Air-fry undisturbed for 6 minutes, or until cooked through. Set the cheese on top of the meat. Continue air-frying undisturbed for 3 minutes, or until the cheese has melted.

4. Use kitchen tongs to divide the meat and cheese layers in the basket between the rolls or buns. Serve hot.

Perfect Burgers

Servings: 3
Cooking Time: 13 Minutes

Ingredients:

- 1 pound 2 ounces 90% lean ground beef
- 1½ tablespoons Worcestershire sauce (gluten-free, if a concern)
- ½ teaspoon Ground black pepper
- 3 Hamburger buns (gluten-free if a concern), split open

Directions:

1. Preheat the air fryer to 375°F .
2. Gently mix the ground beef, Worcestershire sauce, and pepper in a bowl until well combined but preserving as much of the meat's fibers as possible. Divide this mixture into two 5-inch patties for the small batch, three 5-inch patties for the medium, or four 5-inch patties for the large. Make a thumbprint indentation in the center of each patty, about halfway through the meat.
3. Set the patties in the basket in one layer with some space between them. Air-fry undisturbed for 10 minutes, or until an instant-read meat thermometer inserted into the center of a burger registers 160°F (a medium-well burger). You may need to add 2 minutes cooking time if the air fryer is at 360°F.
4. Use a nonstick-safe spatula, and perhaps a flatware fork for balance, to transfer the burgers to a cutting board. Set the buns cut side down in the basket in one layer (working in batches as necessary) and air-fry undisturbed for 1 minute, to toast a bit and warm up. Serve the burgers in the warm buns.

Dijon Thyme Burgers

Servings: 3
Cooking Time: 18 Minutes

Ingredients:

- 1 pound lean ground beef
- ⅓ cup panko breadcrumbs
- ¼ cup finely chopped onion
- 3 tablespoons Dijon mustard
- 1 tablespoon chopped fresh thyme
- 4 teaspoons Worcestershire sauce
- 1 teaspoon salt
- freshly ground black pepper
- Topping (optional):
- 2 tablespoons Dijon mustard
- 1 tablespoon dark brown sugar
- 1 teaspoon Worcestershire sauce
- 4 ounces sliced Swiss cheese, optional

Directions:

1. Combine all the burger ingredients together in a large bowl and mix well. Divide the meat into 4 equal portions and then form the burgers, being careful not to over-handle the meat. One good way to do this is to throw the meat back and forth from one hand to another, packing the meat each time you catch it. Flatten the balls into patties, making an indentation in the center of each patty with your thumb (this will help it stay flat as it cooks) and flattening the sides of the burgers so that they will fit nicely into the air fryer basket.
2. Preheat the air fryer to 370°F.
3. If you don't have room for all four burgers, air-fry two or three burgers at a time for 8 minutes. Flip the burgers over and air-fry for another 6 minutes.
4. While the burgers are cooking combine the Dijon mustard, dark brown sugar, and Worcestershire sauce in a small bowl and mix well. This optional topping to the burgers really adds a boost of flavor at the end. Spread the Dijon topping evenly on each burger. If you cooked the burgers in batches, return the first batch to the cooker at this time – it's ok to place the fourth burger on top of the others in the center of the basket. Air-fry the burgers for another 3 minutes.
5. Finally, if desired, top each burger with a slice of Swiss cheese. Lower the air fryer temperature to 330°F and air-fry for another minute to melt the cheese. Serve the burgers on toasted brioche buns, dressed the way you like them.

Chapter 9 Desserts And Sweets

Fast Brownies

Servings: 4

Cooking Time: 25 Minutes

Ingredients:

- ½ cup flour
- 2 tbsp cocoa
- 1/3 cup granulated sugar
- ¼ tsp baking soda
- 3 tbsp butter, melted
- 1 egg
- ¼ tsp salt
- ½ cup chocolate chips
- ¼ cup chopped hazelnuts
- 1 tbsp powdered sugar
- 1 tsp vanilla extract

Directions:

1. Preheat air fryer at 350ºF. Combine all ingredients, except chocolate chips, hazelnuts, and powdered sugar, in a bowl. Fold in chocolate chips and pecans. Press mixture into a greased cake pan. Place cake pan in the frying basket and Bake for 12 minutes. Let cool for 10 minutes before slicing into 9 brownies. Scatter with powdered sugar and serve.

Coconut-custard Pie

Servings: 4

Cooking Time: 20 Minutes

Ingredients:

- 1 cup milk
- ¼ cup plus 2 tablespoons sugar
- ¼ cup biscuit baking mix
- 1 teaspoon vanilla
- 2 eggs
- 2 tablespoons melted butter
- cooking spray
- ½ cup shredded, sweetened coconut

Directions:

1. Place all ingredients except coconut in a medium bowl.
2. Using a hand mixer, beat on high speed for 3minutes.
3. Let sit for 5minutes.
4. Preheat air fryer to 330°F.
5. Spray a 6-inch round or 6 x 6-inch square baking pan with cooking spray and place pan in air fryer basket.
6. Pour filling into pan and sprinkle coconut over top.
7. Cook pie at 330°F for 20 minutes or until center sets.

Honeyed Tortilla Fritters

Servings: 8
Cooking Time: 10 Minutes
Ingredients:

- 2 tbsp granulated sugar
- ½ tsp ground cinnamon
- 1 tsp vanilla powder
- Salt to taste
- 8 flour tortillas, quartered
- 2 tbsp butter, melted
- 4 tsp honey
- 1 tbsp almond flakes

Directions:

1. Preheat air fryer at 400°F. Combine the sugar, cinnamon, vanilla powder, and salt in a bowl. Set aside. Brush tortilla quarters with melted butter and sprinkle with sugar mixture. Place tortilla quarters in the frying basket and Air Fry for 4 minutes, turning once. Let cool on a large plate for 5 minutes until hardened. Drizzle with honey and scatter with almond flakes to serve.

Fried Oreos

Servings:12
Cooking Time: 7 Minutes
Ingredients:

- 1 Large egg white(s)
- 2 tablespoons Water
- 1 cup Graham cracker crumbs
- 12 Original-size Oreos (not minis or king-size)
- Vegetable oil spray

Directions:

1. Preheat the air fryer to 375°F .
2. Set up and fill two shallow soup plates or small pie plates on your counter: one for the egg white(s), whisked with the water until foamy; and one for the graham cracker crumbs.
3. Dip a cookie in the egg white mixture, turning several times to coat well. Let any excess egg white mixture slip back into the rest, then set the cookie in the crumbs. Turn several times to coat evenly, pressing gently. You want an even but not thick crust. However, make sure that the cookie is fully coated and that the filling is sealed inside. Lightly coat the cookie on all sides with vegetable oil spray. Set aside and continue dipping and coating the remaining cookies.
4. Set the coated cookies in the basket with as much air space between them as possible. Air-fry undisturbed for 6 minutes, or until the coating is golden brown and set. If the machine is at 360°F, the cookies may need 1 minute more to cook and set.
5. Use a nonstick-safe spatula to transfer the cookies to a wire rack. Cool for at least 5 minutes before serving.

Annie's Chocolate Chunk Hazelnut Cookies

Servings: 24

Cooking Time: 12 Minutes

Ingredients:

- 1 cup butter, softened
- 1 cup brown sugar
- ½ cup granulated sugar
- 2 eggs, lightly beaten
- 1½ teaspoons vanilla extract
- 1½ cups all-purpose flour
- ½ cup rolled oats
- 1 teaspoon baking soda
- ½ teaspoon salt
- 2 cups chocolate chunks
- ½ cup toasted chopped hazelnuts

Directions:

1. Cream the butter and sugars together until light and fluffy using a stand mixer or electric hand mixer. Add the eggs and vanilla, and beat until well combined.

2. Combine the flour, rolled oats, baking soda and salt in a second bowl. Gradually add the dry ingredients to the wet ingredients with a wooden spoon or spatula. Stir in the chocolate chunks and hazelnuts until distributed throughout the dough.

3. Shape the cookies into small balls about the size of golf balls and place them on a baking sheet. Freeze the cookie balls for at least 30 minutes, or package them in as airtight a package as you can and keep them in your freezer.

4. When you're ready for a delicious snack or dessert, Preheat the air fryer to 350°F. Cut a piece of parchment paper to fit the number of cookies you are baking. Place the parchment down in the air fryer basket and place the frozen cookie ball or balls on top (remember to leave room for them to expand).

5. Air-fry the cookies at 350°F for 12 minutes, or until they are done to your liking. Let them cool for a few minutes before enjoying your freshly baked cookie.

German Streusel-stuffed Baked Apples

Servings: 4

Cooking Time: 40 Minutes

Ingredients:

- 2 large apples
- 3 tbsp flour
- 3 tbsp light brown sugar
- ⅛ tsp ground cinnamon
- 1 tsp vanilla extract
- 1 tsp chopped pecans
- 2 tbsp cold butter
- 2 tbsp salted caramel sauce

Directions:

1. Cut the apples in half through the stem and scoop out the core and seeds. Mix flour, brown sugar, vanilla, pecans and cinnamon in a bowl. Cut in the butter with a fork until it turns into crumbs. Top each apple half with 2 ½ tbsp of the crumble mixture.

2. Preheat air fryer to 325°F. Put the apple halves in the greased frying basket. Cook until soft in the center and the crumble is golden, about 25-30 minutes. Serve warm topped with caramel sauce.

Baked Apple

Servings: 6

Cooking Time: 20 Minutes

Ingredients:

- 3 small Honey Crisp or other baking apples
- 3 tablespoons maple syrup
- 3 tablespoons chopped pecans
- 1 tablespoon firm butter, cut into 6 pieces

Directions:

1. Put ½ cup water in the drawer of the air fryer.
2. Wash apples well and dry them.
3. Split apples in half. Remove core and a little of the flesh to make a cavity for the pecans.
4. Place apple halves in air fryer basket, cut side up.
5. Spoon 1½ teaspoons pecans into each cavity.
6. Spoon ½ tablespoon maple syrup over pecans in each apple.
7. Top each apple with ½ teaspoon butter.
8. Cook at 360°F for 20 minutes, until apples are tender.

Giant Oatmeal–peanut Butter Cookie

Servings: 4

Cooking Time: 18 Minutes

Ingredients:

- 1 cup Rolled oats (not quick-cooking or steel-cut oats)
- ½ cup All-purpose flour
- ½ teaspoon Ground cinnamon
- ½ teaspoon Baking soda
- ⅓ cup Packed light brown sugar
- ¼ cup Solid vegetable shortening
- 2 tablespoons Natural-style creamy peanut butter
- 3 tablespoons Granulated white sugar
- 2 tablespoons (or 1 small egg, well beaten) Pasteurized egg substitute, such as Egg Beaters
- ⅓ cup Roasted, salted peanuts, chopped
- Baking spray

Directions:

1. Preheat the air fryer to 350°F .
2. Stir the oats, flour, cinnamon, and baking soda in a bowl until well combined.
3. Using an electric hand mixer at medium speed, beat the brown sugar, shortening, peanut butter, granulated white sugar, and egg substitute or egg (as applicable) until smooth and creamy, about 3 minutes, scraping down the inside of the bowl occasionally.
4. Scrape down and remove the beaters. Fold in the flour mixture and peanuts with a rubber spatula just until all the flour is moistened and the peanut bits are evenly distributed in the dough.
5. For a small air fryer, coat the inside of a 6-inch round cake pan with baking spray. For a medium air fryer, coat the inside of a 7-inch round cake pan with baking spray. And for a large air fryer, coat the inside of an 8-inch round cake pan with baking spray. Scrape and gently press the dough into the prepared pan, spreading it into an even layer to the perimeter.
6. Set the pan in the basket and air-fry undisturbed for 18 minutes, or until well browned.
7. Transfer the pan to a wire rack and cool for 15 minutes. Loosen the cookie from the perimeter with a spatula, then invert the pan onto a cutting board and let the cookie come free. Remove the pan and reinvert the cookie onto the wire rack. Cool for 5 minutes more before slicing into wedges to serve.

Fruity Oatmeal Crisp

Servings: 6
Cooking Time: 25 Minutes
Ingredients:

- 2 peeled nectarines, chopped
- 1 peeled apple, chopped
- 1/3 cup raisins
- 2 tbsp honey
- 1/3 cup brown sugar
- ¼ cup flour
- ½ cup oatmeal
- 3 tbsp softened butter

Directions:

1. Preheat air fryer to 380°F. Mix together nectarines, apple, raisins, and honey in a baking pan. Set aside. Mix brown sugar, flour, oatmeal and butter in a medium bowl until crumbly. Top the fruit in a greased pan with the crumble. Bake until bubbly and the topping is golden, 10-12 minutes. Serve warm and top with vanilla ice cream if desired.

Sweet Potato Pie Rolls

Servings:3
Cooking Time: 8 Minutes
Ingredients:

- 6 Spring roll wrappers
- 1½ cups Canned yams in syrup, drained
- 2 tablespoons Light brown sugar
- ¼ teaspoon Ground cinnamon
- 1 Large egg(s), well beaten
- Vegetable oil spray

Directions:

1. Preheat the air fryer to 400°F.
2. Set a spring roll wrapper on a clean, dry work surface. Scoop up ¼ cup of the pulpy yams and set along one edge of the wrapper, leaving 2 inches on each side of the yams. Top the yams with about 1 teaspoon brown sugar and a pinch of ground cinnamon. Fold the sides of the wrapper perpendicular to the yam filling up and over the filling, partially covering it. Brush beaten egg(s) over the side of the wrapper farthest from the yam. Starting with the yam end, roll the wrapper closed, ending at the part with the beaten egg that you can press gently to seal. Lightly coat the roll on all sides with vegetable oil spray. Set it aside seam side down and continue filling, rolling, and spraying the remaining wrappers in the same way.
3. Set the rolls seam side down in the basket with as much air space between them as possible. Air-fry undisturbed for 8 minutes, or until crisp and golden brown.
4. Use a nonstick-safe spatula and perhaps kitchen tongs for balance to gently transfer the rolls to a wire rack. Cool for at least 5 minutes or up to 30 minutes before serving.

Cheese & Honey Stuffed Figs

Servings: 4

Cooking Time: 15 Minutes

Ingredients:

- 8 figs, stem off
- 2 oz cottage cheese
- ¼ tsp ground cinnamon
- ¼ tsp orange zest
- ¼ tsp vanilla extract
- 2 tbsp honey
- 1 tbsp olive oil

Directions:

1. Preheat air fryer to 360°F. Cut an "X" in the top of each fig 1/3 way through, leaving intact the base. Mix together the cottage cheese, cinnamon, orange zest, vanilla extract and 1 tbsp of honey in a bowl. Spoon the cheese mixture into the cavity of each fig. Put the figs in a single layer in the frying basket. Drizzle the olive oil over the top of the figs and Roast for 10 minutes. Drizzle with the remaining honey. Serve and enjoy!

Keto Cheesecake Cups

Servings: 6

Cooking Time: 10 Minutes

Ingredients:

- 8 ounces cream cheese
- ¼ cup plain whole-milk Greek yogurt
- 1 large egg
- 1 teaspoon pure vanilla extract
- 3 tablespoons monk fruit sweetener
- ¼ teaspoon salt
- ½ cup walnuts, roughly chopped

Directions:

1. Preheat the air fryer to 315°F.
2. In a large bowl, use a hand mixer to beat the cream cheese together with the yogurt, egg, vanilla, sweetener, and salt. When combined, fold in the chopped walnuts.
3. Set 6 silicone muffin liners inside an air-fryer-safe pan. Note: This is to allow for an easier time getting the cheesecake bites in and out. If you don't have a pan, you can place them directly in the air fryer basket.
4. Evenly fill the cupcake liners with cheesecake batter.
5. Carefully place the pan into the air fryer basket and cook for about 10 minutes, or until the tops are lightly browned and firm.
6. Carefully remove the pan when done and place in the refrigerator for 3 hours to firm up before serving.

Maple Cinnamon Cheesecake

Servings: 4

Cooking Time: 12 Minutes

Ingredients:

- 6 sheets of cinnamon graham crackers
- 2 tablespoons butter
- 8 ounces Neufchâtel cream cheese
- 3 tablespoons pure maple syrup
- 1 large egg
- ½ teaspoon ground cinnamon
- ¼ teaspoon salt

Directions:

1. Preheat the air fryer to 350°F.

2. Place the graham crackers in a food processor and process until crushed into a flour. Mix with the butter and press into a mini air-fryer-safe pan lined at the bottom with parchment paper. Place in the air fryer and cook for 4 minutes.

3. In a large bowl, place the cream cheese and maple syrup. Use a hand mixer or stand mixer and beat together until smooth. Add in the egg, cinnamon, and salt and mix on medium speed until combined.

4. Remove the graham cracker crust from the air fryer and pour the batter into the pan.

5. Place the pan back in the air fryer, adjusting the temperature to 315°F. Cook for 18 minutes. Carefully remove when cooking completes. The top should be lightly browned and firm.

6. Keep the cheesecake in the pan and place in the refrigerator for 3 or more hours to firm up before serving.

Giant Buttery Oatmeal Cookie

Servings: 4

Cooking Time: 16 Minutes

Ingredients:

- 1 cup Rolled oats (not quick-cooking or steel-cut oats)
- ½ cup All-purpose flour
- ½ teaspoon Baking soda
- ½ teaspoon Ground cinnamon
- ½ teaspoon Table salt
- 3½ tablespoons Butter, at room temperature
- ⅓ cup Packed dark brown sugar
- 1½ tablespoons Granulated white sugar
- 3 tablespoons (or 1 medium egg, well beaten) Pasteurized egg substitute, such as Egg Beaters
- ¾ teaspoon Vanilla extract
- ⅓ cup Chopped pecans
- Baking spray

Directions:

1. Preheat the air fryer to 350°F .

2. Stir the oats, flour, baking soda, cinnamon, and salt in a bowl until well combined.

3. Using an electric hand mixer at medium speed , beat the butter, brown sugar, and granulated white sugar until creamy and thick, about 3 minutes, scraping down the inside of the bowl occasionally. Beat in the egg substitute or egg (as applicable) and vanilla until uniform.

4. Scrape down and remove the beaters. Fold in the flour mixture and pecans with a rubber spatula just until all the flour is moistened and the nuts are even throughout the dough.

5. For a small air fryer, coat the inside of a 6-inch round cake pan with baking spray. For a medium air fryer, coat the inside of a 7-inch round cake pan with baking spray. And for a large air fryer, coat the inside of an 8-inch round cake pan with baking spray. Scrape and gently press the dough into the prepared pan, spreading it into an even layer to the perimeter.

6. Set the pan in the basket and air-fry undisturbed for 16 minutes, or until puffed and browned.

7. Transfer the pan to a wire rack and cool for 10 minutes. Loosen the cookie from the perimeter with a spatula, then invert the pan onto a cutting board and let the cookie come free. Remove the pan and reinvert the cookie onto the wire rack. Cool for 5 minutes more before slicing into wedges to serve.

Home-style Pumpkin Pie Pudding

Servings: 4

Cooking Time: 30 Minutes

Ingredients:

- 1 cup canned pumpkin purée
- ¼ cup sugar
- 3 tbsp all-purpose flour
- 1 tbsp butter, melted
- 1 egg
- 1 orange, zested
- 2 tbsp milk
- 1 tsp vanilla extract
- 4 vanilla wafers, crumbled

Directions:

1. Preheat air fryer to 350°F. Beat the pumpkin puree, sugar, flour, butter, egg, orange zest, milk, and vanilla until well-mixed. Spritz a baking pan with the cooking spray, then pour the pumpkin mix in. Place it in the air fryer and Bake for 11-17 minutes or until golden brown. Take the pudding out of the fryer and let it chill. Serve with vanilla wager crumbs.

Mixed Berry Pie

Servings: 4

Cooking Time: 25 Minutes

Ingredients:

- 2/3 cup blackberries, cut into thirds
- ¼ cup sugar
- 2 tbsp cornstarch
- ¼ tsp vanilla extract
- ¼ tsp peppermint extract
- ½ tsp lemon zest
- 1 cup sliced strawberries
- 1 cup raspberries
- 1 refrigerated piecrust
- 1 large egg

Directions:

1. Mix the sugar, cornstarch, vanilla, peppermint extract, and lemon zest in a bowl. Toss in all berries gently until combined. Pour into a greased dish. On a clean workspace, lay out the dough and cut into a 7-inch diameter round. Cover the baking dish with the round and crimp the edges. With a knife, cut 4 slits in the top to vent.

2. Beat 1 egg and 1 tbsp of water to make an egg wash. Brush the egg wash over the crust. Preheat air fryer to 350°F. Put the baking dish into the frying basket. Bake for 15 minutes or until the crust is golden and the berries are bubbling through the vents. Remove from the air fryer and let cool for 15 minutes. Serve warm.

Honey Apple-pear Crisp

Servings: 4

Cooking Time: 25 Minutes

Ingredients:

- 1 peeled apple, chopped
- 2 peeled pears, chopped
- 2 tbsp honey
- ½ cup oatmeal
- 1/3 cup flour
- 3 tbsp sugar
- 2 tbsp butter, softened
- ½ tsp ground cinnamon

Directions:

1.   Preheat air fryer to 380°F. Combine the apple, pears, and honey in a baking pan. Mix the oatmeal, flour, sugar, butter, and cinnamon in a bowl. Note that this mix won't be smooth. Dust the mix over the fruit, then Bake for 10-12 minutes. Serve hot.

Vanilla Butter Cake

Servings: 6

Cooking Time: 20-24 Minutes

Ingredients:

- ¾ cup plus 1 tablespoon All-purpose flour
- 1 teaspoon Baking powder
- ¼ teaspoon Table salt
- 8 tablespoons (½ cup/1 stick) Butter, at room temperature
- ½ cup Granulated white sugar
- 2 Large egg(s)
- 2 tablespoons Whole or low-fat milk (not fat-free)
- ¾ teaspoon Vanilla extract
- Baking spray (see here)

Directions:

1.   Preheat the air fryer to 325°F (or 330°F, if that's the closest setting).

2.   Mix the flour, baking powder, and salt in a small bowl until well combined.

3.   Using an electric hand mixer at medium speed, beat the butter and sugar in a medium bowl until creamy and smooth, about 3 minutes, occasionally scraping down the inside of the bowl.

4.   Beat in the egg or eggs, as well as the white or a yolk as necessary. Beat in the milk and vanilla until smooth. Turn off the beaters and add the flour mixture. Beat at low speed until thick and smooth.

5.   Use the baking spray to generously coat the inside of a 6-inch round cake pan for a small batch, a 7-inch round cake pan for a medium batch, or an 8-inch round cake pan for a large batch. Scrape and spread the batter into the pan, smoothing the batter out to an even layer.

6.   Set the pan in the basket and air-fry undisturbed for 20 minutes for a 6-inch layer, 22 minutes for a 7-inch layer, or 24 minutes for an 8-inch layer, or until a toothpick or cake tester inserted into the center of the cake comes out clean. Start checking it at the 15-minute mark to know where you are.

7.   Use hot pads or silicone baking mitts to transfer the cake pan to a wire rack. Cool for 5 minutes. To unmold, set a cutting board over the baking pan and invert both the board and the pan. Lift the still-warm pan off the cake layer. Set the wire rack on top of the cake layer and invert all of it with the cutting board so that the cake layer is now right side up on the wire rack. Remove the cutting board and continue cooling the cake for at least 10 minutes or to room temperature, about 30 minutes, before slicing into wedges.

Vegan Brownie Bites

Servings: 10

Cooking Time: 8 Minutes

Ingredients:

- ⅔ cup walnuts
- ⅓ cup all-purpose flour
- ¼ cup dark cocoa powder
- ⅓ cup cane sugar
- ¼ teaspoon salt
- 2 tablespoons vegetable oil
- 1 teaspoon pure vanilla extract
- 1 tablespoon almond milk
- 1 tablespoon powdered sugar

Directions:

1. Preheat the air fryer to 350°F.
2. To a blender or food processor fitted with a metal blade, add the walnuts, flour, cocoa powder, sugar, and salt. Pulse until smooth, about 30 seconds. Add in the oil, vanilla, and milk and pulse until a dough is formed.
3. Remove the dough and place in a bowl. Form into 10 equal-size bites.
4. Liberally spray the metal trivet in the air fryer basket with olive oil mist. Place the brownie bites into the basket and cook for 8 minutes, or until the outer edges begin to slightly crack.
5. Remove the basket from the air fryer and let cool. Sprinkle the brownie bites with powdered sugar and serve.

Apple Crisp

Servings: 4

Cooking Time: 16 Minutes

Ingredients:

- Filling
- 3 Granny Smith apples, thinly sliced (about 4 cups)
- ¼ teaspoon ground cinnamon
- ⅛ teaspoon salt
- 1½ teaspoons lemon juice
- 2 tablespoons honey
- 1 tablespoon brown sugar
- cooking spray

- Crumb Topping
- 2 tablespoons oats
- 2 tablespoons oat bran
- 2 tablespoons cooked quinoa
- 2 tablespoons chopped walnuts
- 2 tablespoons brown sugar
- 2 teaspoons coconut oil

Directions:

1. Combine all filling ingredients and stir well so that apples are evenly coated.
2. Spray air fryer baking pan with nonstick cooking spray and spoon in the apple mixture.
3. Cook at 360°F for 5minutes. Stir well, scooping up from the bottom to mix apples and sauce.
4. At this point, the apples should be crisp-tender. Continue cooking in 3-minute intervals until apples are as soft as you like.
5. While apples are cooking, combine all topping ingredients in a small bowl. Stir until coconut oil mixes in well and distributes evenly. If your coconut oil is cold, it may be easier to mix in by hand.
6. When apples are cooked to your liking, sprinkle crumb mixture on top. Cook at 360°F for 8 minutes or until crumb topping is golden brown and crispy.

INDEX

A

B

C

Printed in Great Britain
by Amazon

11714716R00061